The Only Message That Works

Inspired by Jesus and the teachings of
David Lage

Written & edited by Hannah Ferguson & Amy Melrose

Forward

"The gospel is, heal the sick, raise the dead, cast out devils, get them filled with the Holy Ghost, and speaking in tongues.
 The more you give it out, the more you're going to walk in. I've seen this every day for 20 years."
-Dave Lage

We are commissioned by Jesus to lay hand on the sick, cast out demons, speak in new tongues- to be doers of the Word of God. This book provides the "how-to's", from eternal salvation and infilling of the Holy Spirit to walking in the fullness as a mature Son of God.

⚠ Warning ⚠
To know to do good and not is a sin! Reading this book requires you to step into living out the gospel!

 You are encouraged to look up scripture for yourself where you see it referenced, but not quoted. The original language may differ from the standard translation. Remember that we do not look to anyone but Jesus for our example. Paul did not understand his authority as fully as Jesus did. While we are alive on the earth, we are to see ourselves as Jesus is now, and be untouchable.

(1 John 4:17)

*Reference the distinction between the Old & New Covenants at the end of the book.

Table of Contents

Dear Lord Jesus, come into my heart. Forgive me of my sin. Wash me & cleanse me. Set me free. Jesus, thank You that you died for me. I believe that You are risen from the dead & that You're coming back again for me. Fill me with Your Holy Spirit. Give me passion for the lost. a hunger for the things of God & a holy boldness to preach the gospel of Jesus Christ. I'm saved; I'm born again. I'm forgiven, and I'm on my way to Heaven because I have Jesus inside me! I submit and yield to You, God to work in me to desire and do good today and each day forward for Your pleasure and glory

In The Beginning

Genesis 1:2-3

"The earth was formless and void, and darkness was over the surface of the deep, and the Spirit of God was moving over the surface of the waters. Then God **said**, "Let there be light"; **and there was** light."

All through the creation account, you will see that God *said* and then He *saw*.

Genesis 1:11-12

"Then God **said**, "Let the earth sprout vegetation, plants yielding seed, *and* fruit trees on the earth **bearing fruit after their kind with seed in them**"; and **it was so**. The earth brought forth vegetation, plants **yielding seed after their kind**, and trees bearing fruit **with seed in them, after their kind**; and God **saw** that it was good."

EVERYTHING Produces after its own kind!

You will reproduce *what* *you* are.

Genesis 1:31

"God saw **all** that He had made, and behold, **it was very good**. And there was evening and there was morning, the sixth day."

All that God made **was very good.**

John 6:63

"It is the Spirit who gives life; the flesh profits nothing; the **words** that I have spoken to you are **spirit** and are **life**."

Genesis 1:26-28

"Then God said, "Let Us make man **in Our** *image*, according **to Our** *likeness*; and **let them rule over** the fish of the sea and over the birds of the sky and over the cattle and over all the earth, and **over every creeping thing that creeps on the earth.**" God created man in **His own** *image*, in the *image* of God He created him; male and female He created them. God blessed them; and God said to them, "Be fruitful and multiply, and fill the earth, and **subdue it**; and **rule over** the fish of the sea and over the birds of the sky and over every living thing that moves on the earth."

Hebrew word for *image*: **tselem** meaning resemblance
Hebrew word for *likeness*: **d^emûwth** meaning exact copy

You were made in
God's image.

Psalm 115:16

"The heavens are the heavens of the Lord, But the earth **He has given** to the sons of men."

God gave the earth to man to rule over it.

Thereby, man was given dominion over **all** the earth and directed to subdue it.

Genesis 2:7

"Then the Lord God **formed man of dust** from the ground, and **breathed into his nostrils the breath of life**; and man became a living being."

God duplicated after HIS own kind, when
He breathed life into YOU!

You are an exact replica of God's kind.

John 10:34-35

"Jesus answered them, "Has it not been written in your Law, 'I said, you are gods'? If **he called them gods**, to whom the word of God came (and the Scripture cannot be broken)...""

Jesus quotes the Psalmist, and says that His Father called us gods. God the Father created man to be
the god [ruler] of this world.

Luke 17:6

"And the Lord said, "If you had faith like a mustard seed, you would **say** to this mulberry tree, 'Be uprooted and be planted in the sea' and it would obey you."

Jesus compared faith to a seed.

He demonstrated that 'seeds of faith' are planted by the
words you speak.

Q: Give examples of planting a seed of faith:

_____

_____

_____

_____

_____

_____

_____

_____

_____

_____

Rulership Lost

Genesis 3:1-6
"Now the serpent was more crafty than any beast of the field which the Lord God had made. And he said to the woman, "Indeed, has God said, 'You shall not eat from any tree of the garden'?" <u>The woman said to the serpent,</u> "From the fruit of the trees of the garden we may eat; but from the fruit of the tree which is in the middle of the garden, **God has said**, 'You shall not eat from it or touch it, or you will die.'" <u>The serpent said to the woman,</u> "You surely will not die! For God knows that in the day you eat from it your eyes will be opened, and you will be like God, knowing good and evil." When the woman saw that the tree was good for food, and that it was a delight to the eyes, and that the tree was desirable to make *one* wise, <u>she took from its fruit and ate</u>; and she gave also to **her husband with her**, <u>and he ate.</u>"

God had commanded Adam and his wife to take dominion over all things on the earth, by enforcing God's Word.

Instead, by acting in belief of the serpent's word over God's Word, Eve committed the first sin. Adam followed her knowingly, and gave up man's dominion and handed over rulership to the devil for his illegal reign here on the earth.

2 Corinthians 4:4
"In whose case **the god of this world** has blinded the minds of the unbelieving so that they might not see the light of the gospel of the glory of Christ, who is the image of God."

Q: Paul is referring to satan as 'the god of this world.' How did satan get that position?

_____

_____

Romans 6:16

"Do you not know that when you present yourselves to someone *as* slaves for obedience, <u>you are slaves of the one whom you obey</u>, either of sin resulting in death, or of obedience resulting in righteousness?"

By *"obeying"* the devil, Adam and his wife made themselves slaves to the one whom they were intended to rule over. Against God's will, by the actions of man, sin entered the world and reversed the roles which made the devil ruler.

Romans 5:12

"Therefore, just as <u>through one man sin entered into the world</u>, **and death through sin**, and so **<u>death spread to all men</u>**, because all sinned"

On the day that Adam and Eve ate of the fruit, death was brought into their being, as well as into the whole earth.

Sin **and** sickness are expressions of the *'curse of death'* that man brought himself under.

Sin=_____ Obedience=_____

Genesis 3:17

"Then to Adam He said, "Because you have listened to the voice of your wife, and have eaten from the tree about which I commanded you, saying, "You shall not eat from it," <u>Cursed</u> is the ground because of you; In toil you will eat of it all the days of your life."

Adam and Eve chose knowledge over obedience to God which evicted them from the perfect Garden of Eden that God had made, and sent them into the fallen world.

Q: What consequences come to us today from seeking knowledge over obedience to God?

_____

_____

_____

_____

_____

_____

_____

_____

_____

Q: What was God's original plan for Adam and Eve:

_____

_____

_____

_____

_____

_____

_____

_____

_____

_____

Abraham's Covenant With God

Hebrews 13:8
"Jesus Christ is **the same** yesterday and today and **forever**."

Even though <u>the world changed</u>, **God's Word never changed** and God is not a man, that He should lie. He gave dominion of the earth to those created in His image (man). Therefore it would be illegal for God to take back rulership (which Adam handed over to the devil) to control the world.

God utilized *Covenants* to gain back access into the world.

A Covenant is a promise or a binding agreement between two parties.

A blood covenant is the strongest of covenants, ***requiring up to and unto sacrificing of lives.***

The Covenant God made with Abraham was a blood covenant that meant there was ***nothing*** Abraham and God were not willing to offer up for one another.

This Covenant between God and Abraham gave God access back to this world. Through partnership with man, God could work His plan of salvation to eventually send His own Son to be the sacrifice for all of humanity.

Q: Why was it illegal for God to take rulership when He saw the fall of mankind?

_____

_____

_____

_____

In Genesis 17, God made an eternal covenant with Abraham and his descendants. Abraham, along with all of the people in his day understood what a covenant was. Everything that Abraham owned would be available for God to use, even to the point of his own life, and everything that God had would be available for Abraham.

God <u>had to have a legal right</u> to send His son to the earth. Therefore God made a covenant with Abraham to give up his son, Issac, to make it possible for God to offer up His son, Jesus.

Genesis 22:16-17
"and said, "By Myself I have sworn, declares the Lord, <u>because you have done this thing</u> and have not withheld your son, your only son, indeed I will greatly bless you, and I will greatly multiply your seed as the stars of the heavens and as the sand which is on the seashore; and your **seed shall possess the gate of their enemies**."

Q: How did the blood covenant between God and Abraham provide God access back into this world?

_____

_____

_____

_____

The whole plan of redemption through Jesus hinged on whether a man (Abraham) would believe God.

Genesis 22:8
"Abraham said, "**God will provide for Himself the lamb** for the burnt offering, my son." So the two of them walked on together."

(Hebrews 11:17-19)
Abraham raised the knife to kill his son Isaac, but an angel stopped him. Abraham's <u>willingness to believe God</u> was enough to <u>prove the Covenant</u>. God had provided a ram in the thicket to die in the place of his son, Isaac. This was a shadow of God's Son that would later be sent in place of all mankind.

It was in this Covenant, that the law was created to cover the sins of Abraham's descendants, but it was only temporary.

God still had to deal with man's fallen condition and their nature of sin and death.

The world needed a Savior.

The Seed Of The Woman

Genesis 3:15

"And I will put enmity

Between you and **the woman**,

And between your seed and her **seed**;

He shall bruise you on the head,

And you shall bruise him on the heel."

Even from the beginning, God was speaking of His plan of redemption through sending His son, **Jesus, the seed of the woman**.

Luke 1:38
"And Mary said, "Behold, the bondslave of the Lord; **may it be done to me according to your word**." And the angel departed from her."

Mary was a virgin.
The actual **seed inside her** was not from man, but it **was the Word of God** she *spoke* into existence, "may it be done unto me according to your word." As she made this declaration the Savior of the world was brought forth in her womb.

Q: Why was Mary's verbal declaration necessary for the conception of Jesus?

_____

_____

_____

_____

1 Peter 1:23
"for you have been born again **not** of **seed** which is ***perishable but imperishable***, *that is,* through the living and enduring **word of God**."

John 1:14
"And **the Word became flesh**, and dwelt among us, and we saw His glory, glory as of the only begotten from the Father, full of grace and truth."

Just as in the beginning when God created all things,
The spoken Word of God was made flesh.

Jesus, *the Son of God,* had become *the Son of Man.*

Jesus' Life

Because He was fully man, **Jesus had the dominion, and earthly authority** to cast out devils, and heal the sick, but until **God anointed Jesus with the Holy Ghost,** He didn't have the ability (Power) to do it.

Luke 3:21-23
"Now when all the people were baptized, Jesus was also baptized, and while He was praying, heaven was opened, and **the Holy Spirit descended upon Him** in bodily form like a dove, and a voice came out of heaven, "**You are My beloved Son**, in You I am well-pleased." When He began His ministry, Jesus Himself was about thirty years of age, being, as was supposed, the son of Joseph, the son of Eli,"

Luke 4:5-8
"And the devil took him up and showed him all the kingdoms of the world in a moment of time, and said to him, "To you I will give all this **authority** and their glory, for **it has been delivered to me, and I give it to whom I will**. If you, then, will worship me, it will all be yours." And Jesus answered him, "**It is written**, "'You shall worship the Lord your God, and him only shall you serve.'"

When Jesus chose to **enforce the Word of God** (and NOT obey the devil), He changed everything.
The devil never gained authority over Jesus because Jesus never succumbed to the temptation of the devil.

Romans 6:16
"Do you not know that when you present yourselves to someone *as* slaves for obedience, you are slaves of the one whom you obey, either of sin resulting in death, or of obedience resulting in righteousness?"

Luke 4:14-19

"And Jesus returned to Galilee in the **power** of the Spirit, and news about Him spread through all the surrounding districts. And He *began* teaching in their synagogues and was praised by all. And He came to Nazareth, where He had been brought up; and as was His custom, He entered the synagogue on the Sabbath, and stood up to read. And the book of the prophet Isaiah was handed to Him. And He opened the book and found the place where it was written,

> "The Spirit of the Lord is upon Me,
>
> **Because He anointed Me** to preach the gospel to the poor.
>
> He has sent Me to proclaim release to the captives,
>
> And recovery of sight to the blind,
>
> To set free those who are oppressed,
>
> To proclaim the favorable year of the Lord."

He did **_not_** say, "The Spirit of the Lord is upon Me
Because I am the Son of God."

Q: Jesus said the Spirit of the Lord is upon Him because:

_____

Q: Jesus had to come to earth ***as a*** _____ in order that He would have the _____ God assigned to man.
It was not until He was _____ when _____ that Jesus had the *ability* of God on the earth.

John 5:26-27

"For just as the Father has life in Himself, even so He gave to the Son also to have life in Himself; and He gave Him authority to execute judgment, **because** He is *the* Son of **Man**."

Jesus was the son of God, but He ***did not*** heal *because* He was the *son of God*.

Jesus healed the sick ***because*** He was the son of Man ***anointed*** with the healing power of God.

Acts 10:38

"*You know of* Jesus of Nazareth, how **God anointed Him with the Holy Spirit** and with **power**, and *how* He went about doing good and **healing all** who were oppressed *by the devil,* for **God was with Him**."

Q: Jesus was God in the flesh. So, why would God have to anoint Him with The Holy Ghost and with power?

_____

_____

_____

Philippians 2:6-8

"who, although **He existed in the form of God**, did not regard equality with God a thing to be grasped, but emptied Himself, taking the form of a bond-servant, *and being made in the likeness of men*. Being found in appearance **as a man**, He humbled Himself by becoming obedient to the point of death, even death on a cross."

Mark 14:62

"And Jesus said, "**I am**; and you shall see **the Son of Man** sitting at the right hand of Power, and coming with the clouds of heaven.""

Luke 4:28-37

"And all the people in the synagogue were filled with rage as they heard these things; and they got up and drove Him out of the city, and led Him to the brow of the hill on which their city had been built, in order to throw Him down the cliff. **But passing through their midst, He went His way**. And He came down to

Capernaum, a city of Galilee, and He was teaching them on the Sabbath; and they were amazed at His teaching, for **His message was with authority**.

In the synagogue there was a man possessed by the spirit of an unclean demon, and he cried out with a loud voice, "Let us alone! What business do we have with each other, Jesus of Nazareth? Have You come to destroy us? I know who You are--the Holy One of God!" But <u>Jesus rebuked</u> him, **saying**, "<u>Be quiet and come out of him!</u>" And when the demon had thrown him down in the midst of the people, he came out of him without doing him any harm.

And amazement came upon them all, and they began talking with one another saying, "What is this message? For **with authority <u>and</u> power** He **commands** the unclean spirits and they come out."

And the report about Him was spreading into every locality in the surrounding district."

After Jesus was anointed with The Holy Ghost, He began to cast out devils and heal the sick *for the first time.* Thereafter all of His ministry was with **dominion authority** as the Son of Man, **<u>and</u>** with Holy Ghost **power**!

Jesus walked through an angry mob unharmed. He had the authority to allow or prevent anyone from touching Him.

Despite anger from the religious people of His day, Jesus continued in a ministry of healing the sick, training His disciples, and teaching the people of His coming Kingdom.

Jesus continued to fulfill His purpose - to destroy the works of the devil. (1 John 3:8)

Q: Give examples of when and how Jesus demonstrated His authority and power here on earth.

_____

_____

_____

_____

_____

_____

_____

_____

_____

_____

_____

The Enemy Is Illegal

John 10:10
"The thief comes only to steal and kill and destroy; I came that they may have life, and have *it* abundantly."

John 10:1-2
"Truly, truly, I say to you, <u>he who does not enter by the door</u> into the fold of the sheep, but climbs up some other way, <u>he is a thief</u> and a robber."

In the beginning God established the only legal entry to earth is by being born here. He gave the earth to man.

The devil is here illegally!

Any spirit without a body still does not have ability on this earth unless *man* cooperates with it.

All through the Bible there is a theme of man co-laboring with God. It is important that you know God has given YOU authority and not to allow the devil to deceive you into believing otherwise. The devil wants people sick or crippled to distract, and slow them down from doing God's work. He wants people dead, so that God can no longer work through them here on earth.

You have the legal authority, as well as full access to the anointing of the Holy Ghost to destroy ALL the works of the devil.

The Holy Ghost doesn't have a body. Even the Spirit of God cannot work here on the earth unless somebody willingly receives Him and operates in His anointing. Legally this requires a believer in Jesus filled with the Holy Spirit who is **obedient** to **do** the will of God.

In Luke 4:34 the demon tries to say, "You can't cast me out! You're the Holy One of God, and it's illegal."

 The demon says this because they saw Jesus as **deity** and dominion on earth was given to **man**. The devils did not understand the virgin birth of Jesus being fully God and fully man.Therefore devils challenged Jesus' authority and Jesus responded to the devils every time by commanding them to, "GO!"

Hebrews 10:12-13
"But He, having offered one sacrifice for sins for all time, sat down at the right hand of God, waiting from that time onward until His enemies be made a footstool for His feet."

Q. Give examples of how we make satan God's footstool:

_____

_____

_____

_____

Heaven knows who you are, and hopes you find out.
Hell knows who you are and hopes you don't find out.
The only one who gets to decide that is the one looking back
at you in the mirror every morning.

Jesus Delegates Authority To The Disciples

God needed man to **speak** His Word over the lost, so He could put the saving power to reach the world into motion.

Jesus's disciples followed Him with the expectation that He would train them to do all that He did. Jesus focused on healing the sick, and He trained His disciples' to do the same.

Jesus was able to delegate authority to the disciples based on His knowing that He WOULD pay for **every** healing by the stripes He would take at the whipping post.

Matthew 10:1
"Jesus summoned His <u>twelve</u> disciples and **gave them authority over unclean spirits**, <u>to cast them out</u>, and <u>to heal *every*</u> kind of disease <u>and *every* kind of sickness</u>."

Jesus ordained the twelve disciples, and later, he ordained the seventy disciples. **Every one of them got the same results as Jesus** in cities all over Israel.

Luke 10:17-19
"The **seventy** returned with joy, saying, "Lord, even **the demons are subject to us in Your name**." And He said to them, "<u>I was watching Satan fall from heaven like lightning</u>. **Behold, I have given you authority** to tread on serpents and scorpions, and **over all the power of the enemy**, and nothing will injure you."

It is important to remember that while Jesus was with the disciples they were <u>still in the Old Covenant,</u> operating in *delegated* authority over devils.

Q: Even though the disciples did not have Holy Ghost power in them before the day of Pentecost, describe how they were able to heal and set people free:

_____

_____

_____

_____

_____

_____

_____

John 16:12-13

"I have **many more** things to say to you, but you cannot bear _them_ now. But when He, the Spirit of truth, comes, He will guide you into all the truth; for He will not speak on His own initiative, but whatever He hears, He will speak; and He will disclose to you what is to come."

(Matthew 10:24-25)

Jesus told His disciples it was enough that they be like their master, yet He told them that they would do even greater works than He did.

John 14:12

"Truly, truly, I say to you, he who believes in Me, the works that I do, he will do also; and greater _works_ than these he will do; because I go to the Father."

As the disciples began to do the works of Jesus in the book of Acts, they were able to do even greater works than before. The devil has been defeated. The Holy Spirit of Jesus has now been poured out on ALL flesh! Jesus is seated at the right hand of the Father. All we must do is believe to operate in the greater works that Jesus spoke of.

Q. How can we do the 'greater works' referred to in John 14:12:

_____

_____

_____

_____

_____

_____

_____

Whipping Post & Cross

Jesus came to abolish the Old Covenant and become the perfect Sacrificial Lamb for ALL mankind. Jesus took away all sins, sickness and curses once and for ALL.

Matthew 26:26
"While they were eating, Jesus took *some* bread, and after a blessing, He <u>broke</u> *it* and gave *it* to the disciples, and said, "Take, eat; this is My body".

 The body of Jesus would be broken at the whipping post, and that is when, "By his stripes you <u>*are*</u> healed," became, "By His stripes you <u>*were*</u> healed."

Matthew 26:28
"for this is <u>My blood of the **covenant**</u>, which is poured out for many for forgiveness of sins."

(Galatians 3:13)
 The drink represented the blood of Jesus. He would soon go to die on the tree, breaking EVERY curse once for all.

The New Covenant had now been established.
Christ redeemed us from the curse of the law.

 Jesus called it, My blood *of* the covenant. While the blood of the Old *Covenant* lamb was shed for the **covering** of God's people, the blood that Jesus shed would **destroy** sin and *finish* the covenant that Abraham had started with God.

IT *IS* FINISHED

The blood that was shed paid for ALL sin.
The whipping post healed ALL sickness
The cross broke ALL curses

John 18:6
"So when He said to them, "I am *He,*" they drew back and fell to the ground."

Jesus had to wait for the 300-600 specially trained soldiers to get up off the ground before He could give Himself up to suffer physically in our place. That is how much power that He carried.

(Isaiah 52:14)
When Jesus was whipped, it was **not 39** lashes. He was beaten under Roman law, which meant that there was no limit to His beating. Isaiah says that Jesus was beaten more than any person in history and was unrecognizable as a human being *before* He went to the cross.

2 Corinthians 5:21
"He made Him who knew no sin *to be* sin on our behalf, so that we might become the righteousness of God in Him."

Because He had lived without a single sin, Jesus was able to pay the penalty of sin in our place. He was crushed so that you would be healed, and He died so that you could be born again. This was The Great Exchange of the whipping post for our healing, the blood, for our salvation from sin, and the cross for our salvation from the curse.

Jesus yelled out, "It Is Finished!!" He gave up His spirit to die, and the giant curtain inside the Jewish temple was torn in two.

Q: What was Jesus referring to as being finished?

_____

_____

_____

_____

_____

_____

The Resurrection

Jesus took back the keys (the authority) over earth, death, hell, and the grave.

Revelation 1:18
 I *am* He who lives, and was dead, and behold, I am alive forevermore. Amen. And I have the keys of Hades and of Death.

Until Jesus was raised from the dead, the enemy was still, "the god of this world."

Jesus defeated the devil. It is through Jesus that man's position as ruler here on earth has been restored.

The Old Covenant is *completely finished* and has been replaced with the New Covenant.

Q: Where in scripture does the New Covenant begin?

_____

_____

_____

Q: Upon His resurrection Jesus received ALL authority. How much authority does satan / demons have now here on earth?

_____

_____

_____

Water Baptism

In the Old Covenant, John baptized the people for a symbol of repentance. Now we are in the New Covenant and when people are water baptized in the name of Jesus, the power of the Holy Ghost is always evident. So if you were "baptized" and all that happened was you got wet, then it was an Old Covenant Baptism.

Acts 19:4-6
"On hearing this, they were baptized in the name of the Lord Jesus. When Paul placed his hands on them, the Holy Spirit came on them, and they spoke in tongues and prophesied. There were about twelve men in all."

Acts 8:12
"But when they believed Philip as he preached the things concerning the kingdom of God and the name of Jesus Christ, both men and women were baptized."

Acts 8:13
"Then Simon himself also believed; and when he was baptized he continued with Philip, and was amazed, seeing the miracles and signs which were done."

Acts 22:16
"And now why are you waiting? Arise and be baptized, and wash away your sins, calling on the name of the Lord."

Romans 6:4
"We were therefore buried with him through baptism into death in order that, just as Christ was raised from the dead through the glory of the Father, we too may live a new life."

Q: What 'miracles and signs' are evident in New Covenant Baptisms?

_____

_____

_____

_____

_____

_____

_____

_____

"When we baptize people, we just tell them, "Everything that's not of God stays in the water, and only the New Creation comes out." So, when they make a decision to make Christ their Lord, we speak that into existence over each of them. They cannot come out of the water until they let go of their demons. Their bodies come up healed and whole. We've had kids that were blind in one eye and we didn't even know it. They got new eyes. We've had people that had internal things recreated before they came out of the water. They had brand new parts; kidneys, livers, colons, etc. It's not a ceremony. It's a commitment. 'It's no longer I that live' so the old man dies, and only the new man comes out. We've had people that had demons they thought were the Holy Ghost and you could not pull the people out of the water until they were ready to let go of their demons."
-   Dave Lage

The Great Commission

Jesus did not do one single deliverance/healing after He got His glorified body, because it would be illegal for Him to do so as He no longer has the body of a man.

Jesus delegates His authority to man who believes in Him to fulfill what God has commissioned believers to do.

Matthew 28:18-20
"And Jesus came up and spoke to them, saying, "**All authority** has been given to Me in heaven and on earth. Go therefore and make disciples of all the nations, baptizing them in the name of the Father and the Son and the Holy Spirit, teaching them to observe all that I commanded you; and lo, I am with you always, even to the end of the age."

Mark 16:15-18
"And He said to them, "Go into all the world and preach the gospel to all creation. He who has believed and has been baptized shall be saved; but he who has disbelieved shall be condemned. These signs will accompany those who have believed: in My name they will cast out demons, they will speak with new tongues; they will pick up serpents, and if they drink any deadly *poison,* it will not hurt them; they will lay hands on the sick, and they will recover."

Q: What must man do to operate in the authority of Jesus?

_____

_____

_____

Q: What have believers been commissioned to do?

_____

_____

_____

The Baptism of the Holy Spirit

Luke 24:46-49

"Now He said to them, "These are My words which I spoke to you while I was still with you, that all things which are written about Me in the Law of Moses and the Prophets and the Psalms must be fulfilled." Then He opened their minds to understand the Scriptures, and He said to them, "Thus it is written, that the Christ would suffer and rise again from the dead the third day and that repentance for forgiveness of sins would be proclaimed in His name to all the nations, beginning from Jerusalem. You are witnesses of these things. And behold, I am sending forth the promise of My Father upon you; but you are to stay in the city **_until_** you are clothed with power from on high."

Acts 1:4

"Gathering them together, He commanded them not to leave Jerusalem, but to wait for what the Father had promised, "Which," *He said,* "you heard of from Me; for John baptized with water, but you will be baptized with the Holy Spirit not many days from now."

The exact same power that was with Jesus, empowering Him to be who He was when He walked this earth, is the same power that dwells within those who are baptized with the Holy Spirit. (Acts 10:38)

Acts 1:8

"but you will receive power when the Holy Spirit has come upon you; and you shall be My witnesses both in Jerusalem, and in all Judea and Samaria, and even to the remotest part of the earth."

Acts 2:1-4

"When the day of Pentecost had come, they were all together in one place. And suddenly there came from heaven a noise like a violent rushing wind, and it filled the whole house where they were sitting. And there appeared to them tongues as of fire distributing themselves, and they rested on each one of them. And they were all filled with the Holy Spirit and began to speak with other tongues, as the Spirit was giving them utterance."

Acts 19:2-6

"He said to them, "Did you receive the Holy Spirit when you believed?" And they *said* to him, "No, we have not even heard whether there is a Holy Spirit." And he said, "Into what then were you baptized?" And they said, "Into John's baptism." Paul said, "John baptized with the baptism of repentance, telling the people to believe in Him who was coming after him, that is, in Jesus." When they heard this, **they were baptized in the name of the Lord Jesus**. And when Paul had laid his hands upon them, the Holy Spirit came on them, and they *began* speaking with tongues and prophesying."

Jesus is seated at the right hand of the Father. He no longer has the body of man, and He cannot do anything on this earth unless He does it through a person!
The Holy Spirit - the Spirit of the Living God - resides in those who receive Him.

Q: How does a Believer get baptized with the Holy Spirit?

_____

_____

_____

Q: What is referred to in scripture as 'new tongues'?; when is it given to a believer and for what purpose?

_____

_____

Q: What signs shall follow those who believe in Jesus?

_____

_____

_____

(Acts 3:1-10)
After being filled with the Holy Spirit, Peter and John were heading up to the temple to pray according to their custom. A lame man sitting outside began asking them for money. Instead of money, Peter released the life of God into the man. What manifested was an instant miracle for the whole town to see.

Knowing Who You Are As A Believer
Filled With The Holy Spirit

"The greatest discovery you can ever make is
your identity with God."
- T.L. Osborn

Galatians 2:20
"I have been crucified with Christ; it is no longer I *who* live, *but* Christ *lives in me*; and the life which I now live *in* the flesh I live by faith *in* the Son of God, *who* loved *me* and gave Himself for *me*."

2 Corinthians 5:17
Therefore, if anyone *is* in Christ, *he is* a new creation; old things have passed away; behold, all things have become new.

As a believer in Jesus Christ, filled with the Holy Spirit, we take on a whole new identity. Above all other 'titles', we are known as 'Sons of God'. Jesus is our example and we are to be like Him in ALL ways. The life that Jesus lived in the Bible is the same life that you can live today and greater.

John 14:12
 Truly, truly, I say to you, he who believes in Me, the works that I do, he will do also; and greater *works* than these he will do; because I go to the Father.

1 John 4:17
 By this, love is perfected with us, so that we may have confidence in the day of judgment; because **as He is**, *so also* <u>are we</u> **in this world**.

Jesus had the dominion as the Son of Man

We have the dominion as the Sons of Man

He was the Son of God

We are Now the Sons of God

He was anointed with the Holy Ghost power of God

We have been anointed with the Holy Ghost power of God

He had authority to disallow harm even from people

We have authority to disallow harm even from people

He Destroyed the works of the devil

We destroy the works of the devil

He taught others to do the same

We teach others to do the same

He paid the price for us to have legal right to do the same

We are free because of Jesus' sacrifice

He is in heaven in full power, interceding for us.

We are on earth with full power in us, so that Jesus can live through us.

When Jesus was here on earth, He said He was the light of the world. Now that He is in Heaven, and You are here, YOU are the light of the world. (Matthew 5:14-16)

YOU are Jesus to this world!

Q: What characteristics encompass living by faith as a New Creation in Christ?

_____

_____

_____

_____

_____

_____

_____

_____

_____

_____

2 Corinthians 5:16
 Therefore from now on we recognize no one according to the flesh; even though we have known Christ according to the flesh, yet now **we know *Him in this way no longer***.

His spirit is one with your spirit. (1 Corinthians 6:17)

Before we came to Christ, we were governed by the desires of our flesh, but now we have been recreated in our spirits to be just like Jesus.

(Ephesians 4:17-24)
We are to no longer walk according to our old self and its deceitful desires. We are to walk according to our **new nature** that we have put on in Christ. To understand this new nature we must look to the originator, God himself.

We face a *defeated enemy*! Jesus made an open show of the devil, triumphing over him. We are the devil's masters! There is no battle for us as the body of Christ, we need only enforce the victorious position that Jesus provided us and put the enemy under foot to be made God's footstool.

For a Believer, there are no 'big devils and little devils.'
They are ALL defeated.

Hebrews 10:12-13
"but He, having offered one sacrifice for sins for all time, sat down at the right hand of God, waiting from that time onward until His enemies be made a footstool for His feet."

Q: What must we do to make God's enemy (satan) His footstool?

_____

_____

_____

_____

_____

_____

"Over 30 years ago, I was sitting in my truck, and looked outside. I was special ops trained, but fear hit me where I couldn't hardly move. There was the devil, standing at my window. On the other side Jesus appeared to me. At that time I didn't know which one I was more afraid of. I was between Heaven and Hell, and I'm waiting for Jesus to do something. I was expecting a big blow up, but Jesus bent over and said to me, "Tell him to leave in My name." Later, I was reading that Kenneth Hagin Sr. had that same vision. He said, "Why ain't you doing something about all these devils?" Jesus said, "I can't." The video Charles Capps 58 (on authority) nails it. You have to be born with blood in your veins to have dominion on earth. Jesus has all authority in heaven and on earth, but He can't use it because He's no longer flesh and blood. For some reason that's so hard for Christians to get because they've been brainwashed by the church. "Oh, the sovereignty of God…" "It's up to God." The Bible says it's up to us! He gave US, people, authority and dominion over the earth, and He told us to subdue it, and take dominion over it.

So, after Jesus spoke that truth to me in the truck, and I got that revelation, I watched the devil shape shift smaller, and smaller until he completely went away."

-Dave Lage

"You're worthy. You need to think more highly of yourself.
If you don't think highly enough of yourself,
you won't step out in faith."
-Dave Lage

The Gospel is:

Romans 1:16

"For I am not ashamed of **the gospel**, for <u>it **is** the **power** of God for salvation *to*</u> *<u>everyone who believes,</u>* to the Jew first and also to the Greek."

The Gospel *IS* the Power of God
that saves people from the works of the devil.

Matthew 10:7-8

"As you go, <u>preach **this** message</u>: 'The kingdom of heaven is near.' <u>Heal the sick</u>, <u>raise the dead</u>, <u>cleanse the lepers</u>, <u>drive out demons</u>. Freely you have received; freely give."

Jesus' ministry was mostly made up of **healing the sick**, and He commanded His disciples to do the same.

Luke 10:8-9

"Whatever city you enter and they receive you, eat what is set before you; and <u>heal</u> those in it who are sick, and <u>say</u> to them, 'The kingdom of God has come near to you.'"

The true gospel of Jesus is ***always*** a demonstration of God's power.

1 Corinthians 2:4

"and **my message** and **my preaching** were not in persuasive words of wisdom, but in ***demonstration of the Spirit and of power***"

Q: Give examples of Sons of God demonstrating God's power.

_____

_____

_____

_____

_____

_____

_____

_____

_____

_____

Do Not Add To Or Take Away From Jesus (The Word)

1 Timothy 1:3-7
"As I urged you on my departure to Macedonia, you should stay on at Ephesus to **instruct** certain **men not to teach false doctrines** or devote themselves to myths and endless genealogies, which promote speculation rather than the stewardship of God's work, which is by faith.
The goal of our instruction is the love that comes from a pure heart, a clear conscience, and a sincere faith. Some have strayed from these ways and turned aside **to empty talk**. They want to be teachers of the law, but they do not understand what they are saying or that which they so confidently assert."

Revelation 22:14-15
"Blessed are those who wash their robes, so that they may have the right to the tree of life and that they may enter the city by the gates. Outside are the dogs and sorcerers and the sexually immoral and murderers and idolaters, and **everyone who loves and practices falsehood."**

There is ONE gospel in the New Covenant.

Galatians 1:6-10
"I am amazed that you are so quickly deserting Him who called you by the grace of Christ, for a different gospel; which is *really* not another; only there are some who are disturbing you and want to distort the gospel of Christ. **But even if we, or an angel from heaven, should preach to you a gospel contrary to what we have preached to you, he is to be accursed!** As we have said before, so I say again now, if any man is preaching to you a gospel contrary to what you received, he is to be accursed! For am I now seeking the favor of men, or of God? Or am I striving to please men? If I were *still trying to please men*, I would not be a bond-servant of Christ."

God's position is that one should be "accursed" for teaching a different Gospel than the one that Jesus demonstrated with power. It may please men, but false gospels will actually keep people away from God.

Q: What does scripture tell us about seeking the favor of man?

_____

_____

_____

Any man *who calls himself a brother*, but is living a lifestyle of rebellion to God, leading people astray should not be listened to, or associated with.
Those are God's words.
(1 Corinthians 5:11-13)

Matthew 16:12
"Then they understood that He was not telling them to *beware* of the leaven used in bread, but of **the teaching** of the Pharisees and Sadducees."

The Pharisees teaching is non-action, religious traditions and **words with no power.**

1 Corinthians 2:2
"For I determined to know nothing among you except **Jesus Christ**, and Him crucified."

The message of the gospel is **Jesus Christ**.
Too many churches teach everything BUT Jesus. If a teaching enables you to *not* BE like Jesus in all ways, throw it out.

Let's Keep It Simple, Sons.
STAY AWAY from **false doctrines**.

Q: What does scripture say happens to us if we 'Add to or take away from' the Word?
(Jesus is the Word made flesh)

_____

_____

_____

"This man we met would never say the name of Jesus. He'd call the spirit that talked to him, "Lord." We got him off his death bed several times. He was at our house, and we'd get the sickness off of him, but he wouldn't get out of bed. The third day he was there he said, "Dave, Jesus has been at the foot of my bed. Why won't he heal me?"
I looked up, and what was at the end of his bed looked like a Grim Reaper devil. I told the man, "Say, 'Jesus' loud and bold three times." Each time I'd encourage him, "Louder!" After his third time speaking the name of Jesus, he exclaimed, "It's a devil!" I'd been telling him that for years.
No matter what they say, these people put their experience ahead of scripture. Jesus is the Word. He said it was all finished. Anybody that doesn't tell you it's all finished isn't from heaven."
- Dave Lage

(2 Corinthians 11:14)
We've seen too many examples of this sort of thing taking people out, even in church leadership. People call their demons, "God." This 'god' will influence them to do things that the Jesus of the Bible would NEVER do, and it brings death spiritually and physically. Do not be looking for anything new. The gospel that's written will never change.

Jesus + <u>Nothing</u> = Everything.
You will know them by their fruits. (Matthew 7:15-20)

From The Old To The New
(Where Are You Seated? Slave Or King)

The difference between an Old Covenant mindset, and the New Covenant mindset in any area of your life is this:

Old Covenant = looking forward for God to fulfill a promise in the future

New Covenant = looking at what God has *already done* over 2,000 years ago as finished through Jesus

(Hebrews 1:1-4)
Jesus is the perfect reflection of God's character, and will. Jesus taught the truth, and His life was a reflection of truth. The Old Covenant did not fully reflect God's character, it was only a shadow of what was to come. God had to deal with man legally, with justice and holiness in line with His nature. Later, Jesus was able to bring mercy and redemption.

The Old Covenant Mindset is deceived into looking for a mediator to speak to God, and will always be trying to *earn* what God has *freely given*! They will be **looking *for God to do something*, when God has already done all that He needs to do!**

(Hebrews 8:6)
The New Covenant is truth for us to live by today established on Jesus' having finished it ALL!

It is crucial that you understand the difference between the Old and New Covenants as it serves as the filter of your general outlook on the entire Bible and the foundation from which your **actions** as a Believer spring forth.

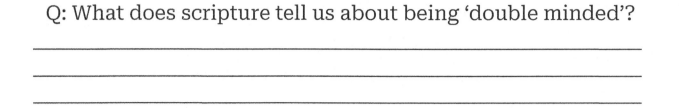

Q: What does scripture tell us about being 'double minded'?

_____

_____

_____

The devil uses fear built into religious traditions to cause people to be too afraid to do anything without express permission from their Pastor. If your Pastor is not equipping you, and sending you out to do the works of Jesus, then He is not a Biblical Pastor. (Ephesians 4:11-16) Never be afraid to do the will of God.

The permission to obey God's Word is built into His instruction.

Most people seem to be waiting on God to tell them specifically what to do and when to do it, rather than realizing that God has already told us what to do and given us examples of how to do it. In any company, the most valuable employee is not the one that constantly has to be told exactly what to do. It is the one that finds what needs to be done and does it without being told. Any specifics we may need will be given AS WE GO, and not UNTIL WE GO.

Go = (take action/make a demand on God's power)

(John 14:11-13)
We accomplish the will of the Father just like Jesus. He never asked God for healing, or power of any kind.

The word **ask** can be translated - "whatever you ***make a demand on*** in my name."

Many things once written in the Old Testament are no longer true today. You would not go for a drive on the left side of the road just because we used to be a British colony years ago. Those laws are opposite of our laws today. Similarly, the Old Testament laws were removed long ago. They are now only a part of history. Today, we have the New Covenant. 1 Corinthians chapter 2 shows a great comparison between the application of Old Testament writings before and after the cross.

Paul quotes Isaiah 64:4 in 1 Corinthians 2:9-10

"'But as it is written, Eye hath not seen, nor ear heard, Neither have entered into the heart of man, The things which God hath prepared for them that love him.' **But God hath revealed *them* unto us by his Spirit**: for the Spirit searcheth all things, yea, the deep things of God."

In the Old Covenant, the things of God were a mystery. They were unknown, but now that mystery has been revealed. We DO know God's will for us. Paul goes on to say that the only way a person could know what is inside of God, is to have His own Spirit in them. That was an impossibility before, but now, because of what Jesus did, we have the Spirit of God inside of us, and are able to know ALL things in God. That is the new reality that we walk in since the shift of the covenants.

Then, in 1 Corinthians 2:16 Paul quotes Isaiah 40:13
"For who hath known the mind of the Lord, that he may instruct him? **But** we have the mind of Christ."

Scripture states that in the past it was one way, but now, because we have received the **Spirit** of God, we have the **mind** of God available to us.

Q: How does a Believer have the mind of Christ?

_____

_____

_____

_____

God has provided us with what we need to be like Christ in all ways. Today, He is conforming us to the image of His Son by His Spirit. We must grow up in every way to be like Jesus now.

Romans 12:1-2)

We are not to follow the ways of the world, but to be transformed from one way of being to another by the renewal of our mind. The word, "renew" means to make something new and fresh. If you are born again, and filled with the Holy Spirit, Jesus has given you a fresh, perfect <u>Spirit</u>- His! It is your job to put away the carnal mind, and override it with the actions of the <u>mind</u> of Christ. With His mind in full operation inside of you, you will have a perfect, transformed <u>body</u>. Then, with your spirit, mind, and body in alignment with God, your entire life will be a perfect reflection of God because you will be in submission to Him, enabling His power to flow through you at all times.

Q: Describe the difference in Old Covenant "begging" prayers vs. New Covenant declarations:

_____

_____

_____

_____

_____

_____

_____

_____

_____

_____

Atonement vs. Redemption

Atonement only served to *temporarily* **cover over** sin in the Old Covenant. What Jesus did **redeemed** us, and defeated the nature of sin completely on our behalf. (Hebrews 9:11-14)

(Romans 3:23)
All **have** sinned. That is **past tense**. If you are saved, then even though you *have sinned*, you are no longer a *sinner*. **You are a Saint.** You are a Son of God that may make a mistake (sin) occasionally. However, you no longer have a sin nature.

When Jesus paid for your redemption, He made provision for both salvation from sin *and* salvation from bodily sickness.

In English Bibles, salvation has been translated:

In Matthew 9:22 **"cured"**   In John 11:12 **"recover"**   In James 5:15 **"restore"**
In Luke 9:56 **"save"**   In Acts 14:9 **"healed"**

It is all the *same word*.
Jesus' salvation means absolute
deliverance from *all* harm and lack.
That is the good news!

(Psalm 103:2-6)
Do not forget **all** the benefits of the Lord. He forgives **_all_** our sins and heals **_all_** our diseases. Forgiveness and healing have been coupled together in this verse. If you believe the Bible, and you believe that all sins have been paid for according to God's will, then you must also believe that all sickness has been paid for. You cannot have one truth without the other.

Jesus always attributed sickness to a work of the devil. (John 10:10) Not once did He ever say: "My Father has given you this sickness to teach you something." One of God's names states that He is our healer, He is not our oppressor.

Sickness is *always* a work of the devil.

Isaiah 53:4-5
"Surely our **griefs (choliy)** He Himself **bore, (Nasa)**
And our **sorrows (mak'ob)** He **carried; (Sabal)**
Yet we ourselves esteemed Him stricken,
Smitten of God, and afflicted.
But He was pierced for our transgressions,
He was crushed for our iniquities;
The chastening for our well-being *fell* upon Him,
And by His scourging we are healed."

(Isaiah 53:11-12)
The Hebrew words sabal and nasa are synonyms and in plain English language they mean "To carry for someone something so that they do not need to carry it." So when it says that He would "nasa" or "sabal" our sickness and our sin, that means He would carry for us what we deserved **so that we don't need to carry it.**

(Matthew 8:14-17)
 Matthew was quoting from Isaiah 53:4, but where the words "griefs" and "sorrows" were used, he replaced them with "illnesses" and "diseases."
 Matthew concluded that the casting out of demons as well as the healing of physical diseases is what the prophetic word in Isaiah was about. The Hebrew word for "griefs" is "choliy," and has the **primary** definition of *sickness*. Matthew was a first century Jew who understood the Hebrew word "choliy" better than any English speaker today. The context of its fulfillment leaves no room for speculation.

He took our illnesses and bore our diseases.

(1 Peter 2:24)
 We can see that Peter restated Isaiah 53:5-6. It was not mis-quoted. Peter had witnessed to the fact that Isaiah 53:4 had been **fulfilled**. He is showing us that something had changed since the time Isaiah spoke out this prophetic word.

Isaiah said: "But he was wounded for our transgressions; he was crushed for our iniquities"

Peter said: "He himself bore our sins in His body on the tree."

Isaiah said: "with His stripes we are healed"

Peter said: "By his wounds you have been healed."

Q: Describe the nature of God:

_____

_____

_____

_____

_____

_____

_____

_____

As a believer in Jesus Christ,
filled with the Holy Spirit, you no longer have a sin nature.

You are a new creation with God's nature!

Total Redemption

It was because of Adam's disobedience that sin and the effects of sin came to all men. Being cut off from the spirit of God caused mankind to adopt the worldly identity of satan as everything comes out of union with God.

(Romans 5:12-14)
Adam represented all of mankind, and allowed sin to come into the world. Adam was a type of Jesus, because Jesus would represent all of mankind and bring mankind into a new way of life, free from sin. Sin brought death into our world. **This means that death was never God's plan.** Usually people think of death as a normal part of life but it was not what God intended for us when He created us. Death is the final destination of sickness. In other words, sin/sickness left untreated will result in death.

Q: Sin leads to _____ which leads to death.

(Romans 8:9-11)
In Christ, even if the body is dead because of sin, the Spirit is life because of righteousness. The Spirit that raised Jesus from the dead lives in you, and will also give life to your physical body. If you are born again, you have the Spirit of God within you *always* because He has taken up residence in you.

God does not want visitation rights, He wants habitation rights.

God's plan was to bring us back into right standing with Him so that He could make us one with His spirit again. In doing this, God has taken up habitation in all those who believe. God's desire is that we should be completely reconciled to Him, in Spirit, Soul and Body.

- Reconciliation of the Spirit = The Rebirth.
- Reconciliation of the soul = The Renewing of the mind.
- Reconciliation of the body = The Healing of the physical body.

If Adam's disobedience could bring a spiritual death that resulted in people physically dying,
then the physical and the spiritual are connected, and **_not_** disconnected as many might believe.

This is the Law of sin and death which was ushered in by Adam and that Paul speaks about in the book of Romans.

(Romans 8:2-4)
 If the physical act of disobedience could bring about spiritual death, resulting in physical death, one act of physical obedience on the cross, through Jesus Christ, could restore our spiritual condition, bringing about a restoration to our physical bodies.

When a Son speaks in line with the Word of God,
Heaven is in agreement, and Hell has received its marching orders.
The captives go free!

Q: Where is Jesus, the Holy Spirit, and the Father?

_____

_____

_____

Paul's Thorn

Cambridge online Dictionary For, "Thorn In Your Side"
<u>Someone or something that continually causes problems for you</u>:
"Media censorship has been a thorn in the side of those practicing freedom of speech."

Looking at the same idiom from the Old Testament you can see that it refers to a *people group* or a *person* who continually causes problems for someone. English speakers would use the term 'pain in the neck.'
The idiom "Thorn in the flesh" <u>has never once been used to refer to a sickness or disease</u>, but it has <u>always</u> referred to a person, or a group of people who are continually bothersome.

Numbers 33:55
"But if you do not drive out the inhabitants of the land from before you, then it shall come about that those whom you let remain of them *will become* as pricks in your eyes and as <u>thorns in your sides</u>, and they will trouble you in the land in which you live."

(In Joshua 23:13 the thorn in the side is also mentioned, describing a people group)

Paul was a scholar of Old Testament scriptures and was familiar with the idiom, "thorn in the side." Paul would often speak about the hardships that he faced because of the gospel. <u>Not one of those hardships ever mentioned **sickness**</u>.

(1 Corinthians 4:10-13)
Paul was weak. (Not sick, most likely from being beaten up.)
He was disgraced, hungry, thirsty, poor, **buffeted**, and reviled.

Q: What does the idiom 'Thorn in the flesh' really mean?

_____

_____

The Hardships That Paul Faced:

1. Acts 9:23 - Jews determined to kill Paul right after his conversion.
2. Acts 9:26-29 - He was hindered in joining the Christians.
3. Acts 13:6-12 - He was opposed by satan.
4. Acts 13:44-49 - He was opposed by Jews in a mob.
5. Acts 13:50 - He was expelled out of Antioch in Pisidia.
6. Acts 14:1-5 - He was mobbed and expelled from Iconium.
7. Acts 14:6-9 - He fled to Lystra and Derbe where he was stoned and left for dead.
8. Acts 19:8 - He was disputing continually with false brethren.
9. Acts 16:12-40 - He was beaten and jailed at Philippi.
10. Acts 17:1-10 - He was mobbed and expelled from Thessalonica.
11. Acts 17:10-14 - He was mobbed and expelled from Berea.
12. Acts 18:1-23 - He was mobbed at Corinth.
13. Acts 19:23-31 - He was mobbed at Ephesus.
14. Acts 20:3 - There was a plot against his life by the Jews.
15. He was seized by Jews, mobbed, tried in court five times, and suffered other hardships.

When the Scripture talks about infirmities, it is not necessarily talking about sicknesses. Many people have in mind that because sick people go to the infirmary, then they must have an infirmity. This is why they get the mistaken idea that this word "infirmity" means sickness. But upon closer investigation we find that it does not necessarily mean sickness at all. We will find that infirmity is better translated as weakness than sickness. Some Bible translations have, in-fact, gone as far as to translate it into weaknesses rather than infirmities. (E.g. 2 Corinthians 12:4-5)

Paul describes what he considers weakness as being beaten, stoned, shipwrecked, and given lashes, but none of the explanations refer to sicknesses.

2 Corinthians 12:7
"So to keep me from becoming conceited because of the surpassing greatness of the revelations, a <u>thorn</u> was given me in the flesh, a <u>messenger of Satan</u> to <u>harass</u> me, to keep me from becoming conceited."

The <u>messenger harassing comes from *Satan*</u>, **not from God**.
The Word Harass means, "to be subjected to aggressive pressure or intimidation." In the Greek language, this word means to punch, beat, strike, buffet, or trouble. It is an athletic term taken from the boxing match.

2 Corinthians 12:8-10
"Concerning this I implored the Lord three times that it might leave me. And He has said to me, "**My grace is sufficient for you**, <u>for power is perfected in weakness.</u>" Most gladly, therefore, I will rather boast about my weaknesses, so that the power of Christ may dwell in me. Therefore I am well content with weaknesses, with insults, with distresses, with persecutions, with difficulties, for Christ's sake; for when I am weak, then I am strong."

Paul did not understand his authority in Christ, though God constantly spoke this identity into him. God told Paul that <u>His grace</u>, (divine ability) in Paul was <u>sufficient to overcome every problem</u>. Paul had the answer inside of him to be untouchable from persecution like Jesus, but he did not learn to use it until near the end of his ministry.

Paul did not suffer *sickness*, <u>only hardship and persecution</u>.

Many people believe that Paul had an eye disease. The evidence does not support this idea.

(Galatians 6:11)
Some interpret large letters as in Large letters, saying that Paul could hardly see, but Paul was talking about the lengthy letters that he *wrote*!

(Galatians 4:13-16)
 In Acts 14:19 Paul had just been <u>stoned to death</u>. His eyes were most likely puffed up, cut up and badly bruised.
 In Acts 19:12 people carried handkerchiefs or aprons from Paul to the sick for healing. Nowhere in the Bible do we have a sick man healing the sick. If Paul had a contagious condition like some say, would people really have been willing to even touch his clothing? Idioms are used to emphasize a point, and Paul used them in examples such as in Galatians 6:15 'For I testify to you that, if possible, you would have gouged out your eyes and given them to me.'
Today we would use the idiom 'I would give my right arm to help you.'

Q: Did Paul ever overcome any of satan's messengers?

_____

_____

_____

(Acts 13:6-12)
 A Roman governor, (proconsul) Sergius Paulus wanted to hear more about the word of God, but the false prophet, Bar-Jesus (messenger of Satan) opposed Paul so as to divert Sergius from the faith. Paul rebuked Bar-Jesus, and used his authority to declare him blind for a time. After Paul had shut up the false prophet, Sergius Paulus believed.

(Philippians 3:12-16)
 Paul did <u>not</u> have a revelation of his authority in Christ, but he desired to walk in the fulness. He began to take dominion over trouble-makers later, but **our ultimate example is Jesus**, and He NEVER backed down to a devil.

No one could harm Jesus until He allowed them to!

What About Job?

Job was in a different Covenant than you are in today!

The book of Job has been misinterpreted so that many people believe that God randomly chooses people to test them with trials and misfortune. You, and the people around you were <u>NEVER</u> designed by God to be like Job. You were designed by God with the destiny of being like Jesus, who overcame the temptations of the devil.

James 1:12-14
"Blessed is a man who perseveres under trial; for once he has been approved, he will receive the crown of life which *the Lord* has promised to those who love Him. <u>Let no one say</u> when he is tempted, "<u>I am being tempted by God</u>"; for <u>God cannot</u> be tempted by evil, and He Himself **does not tempt anyone**. But each one is tempted when he is carried away and enticed by *his own lust*."

(James 5:10-11)
The Lord was full of compassion and merciful to Job.

Temptation **always** comes from the devil

Job 1:12
"Then the Lord said to Satan, "Behold, all that he (Job) has is in your power, only do not put forth your hand on him." So Satan departed from the presence of the Lord."

Most people **misinterpret** verse 12 to mean that "*God turned Job over to the Devil.*" That is not consistent with the word of God. **Due to the fall of man** Job was already under the power of the devil.

God did not put Job in the devil's hands.

(Job 1:13-16)
 A general belief in those days was that everything that happened came from God.
So, the servant told Job, "The fire of God fell from heaven," because it came from
the sky. However, it was actually the work of the devil. Lightning struck a pond
where all of the sheep were watering, and it killed them all. The devil is the one
who brings destruction through storms.
 In Mark 4:36-40 Jesus calmed the storm. Jesus does not work against God.
Calming the storm was destroying the works of the devil. (1 John 3:8)

Jesus never destroyed God's work.
Jesus only destroyed the works of the devil.

(Job 1:19-22)
 Again, the elements of nature destroyed Job's property. Job's assessment of what
was happening was, "The Lord gave and the Lord has taken away," but this **was
not a true statement**.
 If you were told that it was raining cats and dogs falling from the sky yesterday,
you could correctly report that this had been said. However, the statement
reported would be untrue as the sky did not produce cats and dogs. The Bible has
accurately recorded what Job actually said about his situation, but just because
Job said it, does not make it the truth.

 God has been accused of doing many things to Job. What God actually did was
restore Job's fortunes, and families.

(Job 42:10)
 When Job prayed for his friends, the Lord was able to return the loss of his
fortunes and multiplied them so that it was double of what he had lost. God was
the one that restored everything back to Job with an increase of 100%. The Devil
was the one that took everything from Job.

Q: What effect did the devil have on Job?

_____

_____

_____

_____

_____

_____

Q: What effect did God have on Job?

_____

_____

_____

_____

_____

_____

The Sovereignty Of God

"God is in control" is a common misconception.

God is <u>not</u> in control, He *is* sovereign.

<u>Sovereignty</u> (noun): supreme power or authority. the authority of a state to govern itself or another state. a self-governing state.

(Genesis 1:26-28)
God ***sovereignly*** decided to make mankind and ***to give them dominion*** over the earth and all that was in it. Adam was given authority over every thing that lived in the sea, that flew in the sky, over livestock, over everything including plants and creeping things, like snakes and insects.

Psalm 8:5-6
"Yet **You have made him a little lower than God**,
And <u>You crown him with glory and majesty</u>!
You make him to rule over the works of Your hands;
<u>You have put **all things under his feet**.</u>"

God made *Man* the **highest ranking spiritual authority** under God.

God knows beforehand who will choose Him. He is not choosing who He wants in His Kingdom. God *foreknowing* how something is going to work out, is *not* the same thing as God orchestrating every thing that happens in your life.

(Romans 8:26-29)
If you love God, you are called according to His purpose, and God works all things together for **good**. <u>God does not create or cause bad things to happen to you.</u> Bad

circumstances can come about due to attacks from the enemy or consequences from man's poor decisions. God can fix any mess if you allow Him to work through you. When you don't know what to do, just pray in tongues! The Spirit intercedes on your behalf according to the will of God.

God is not interested in *controlling* you
or your circumstances.
God is interested in giving *you choices.*

Scriptures plainly state God's will for mankind. However, the will of God is not automatically done as He gave ***us free will***.

We have to **choose** God's will for our lives.

(2 Peter 3:9)
God does not wish for *anyone* to perish. God wants ALL to reach repentance. God's will is not automatically done, many are not choosing to repent and follow Him, therefore they are perishing.

Ephesians 5:17
"So then do not be foolish, but <u>understand what the will of the Lord is</u>."
We must choose to put our faith in Christ. <u>We choose</u> to receive His salvation. God is urging <u>us</u> to choose life, not death.

Deuteronomy 30:19
"<u>I call heaven and earth to witness against you</u> today, **that I have set before you life and death, the blessing and the curse.** So choose life in order that you may live, you and your descendants,"

Q: What is God's will for our lives?

_____

_____

_____

_____

_____

_____

When a King decides to make a law about anything, he is making a decree which is made known to all the citizens of his kingdom. The King's citizens did not vote on it or have a say in the new law. The King's decision is his _sovereign_ right.

Each citizen, in the privacy of his own home, would choose each day whether or not to obey the law. This is where the interpretation of sovereignty is often misused. Sovereignty does not mean that the King controls every person. He does not have some mystical power that causes the citizens to obey his will, whether or not they wanted to. If a person chose to reject the law of the King, then that person would face the consequences.

God has chosen to write His will in the scriptures,
however it is up to **you** to choose whether or not to obey it.

"We've been waiting on God, and He's been waiting on us. Who do you suppose is late?"

-Dave Lage

Dealing With Generational Curses

There is a misconception in the church today which blames sin, sickness/disease and personal struggles on *'generational curses'*. It is believed that, once these curses are dealt with, all the problems and negative symptoms will go away. When issues persist or new problems develop, people dig further into their past, hoping to find some 'curses' that will explain the reason for their situation. These people discount being responsible *themselves* and instead blame generational curses for their predicament. Jesus never got people free by digging up Generational Curses from their past. He said in Luke 9 that anyone who looks back is not fit for the Kingdom. This is an important principle which we can see all throughout the Bible.

Generational sin is <u>not the same</u> as Generational Curses!

Generational <u>Sin</u> is a sinful behavior that has been learned through the lifestyle of parents. It is an ongoing sin, like fear, that embraces the family's everyday life, i.e. often parents who are fearful, pass it on to their children and they, in turn, learn to be fearful. Yet God tells us that <u>He has not given us a spirit of Fear</u>.

Generational curses are an old covenant belief first mentioned when the law was given by Moses. It became popular in Israel, which gave rise to justification among the people to judge people according to the sin of their parents, or even grandparents. This idea has left the church blaming sinful behavior and what happens to them on generations before them, and not <u>taking responsibility for their own actions</u>.

God was unhappy with Israel judging others based on parent's sins or justifying their behavior on the disobedience of their parents.
He *details* this in **Ezekiel 18**, Which gives <u>no room for misinterpretation</u> that **Generational Curses have ended**.

Ezekiel 18:1-4

"Then the word of the Lord came to me, saying, "What do you mean by using this proverb concerning the land of Israel, saying,

'The fathers eat the sour grapes,
But the children's teeth are set on edge'?

   "As I live," declares the Lord God, "**you are surely not going to use this proverb in Israel anymore.** Behold, all souls are Mine; the soul of the father as well as the soul of the son is Mine. The soul who sins will die."
- also see Jeremiah 31:29-30

This is a clear scripture showing the truth that our forefathers' sins **do not affect us**. God demonstrates this by showing them that the sinner themselves face punishment/death and **not** the one who does *not* sin.

(Ezekiel 18:5-9)
 This scripture is describing a good person who is pleasing to God. God declares that the good person lives.

(Ezekiel 18:10-13)
 Now we have the son of the good person. This son **does not follow in his father's footsteps**. He is sinful. His blood is on himself, which means he is responsible for his own consequence.

(Ezekiel 18:14-17)
 Finally, we have the third generation. **This son is the son of a sinful person**. Traditionally we have been taught that his father's sin should be visited onto him. However, this son is a good person. So, what happens?

(Ezekiel 18:18-20)
 The bad father died for his own sin, because he did wrong. The good son does not suffer punishment for his father's sin. Likewise the father will not suffer punishment for the son's sin.

Righteousness will be on the righteous person.
Wickedness will be on the wicked person.

(Ezekiel 18:21-24)
 If a <u>wicked person repents</u>, then his **sins will be forgiven** him. If a <u>righteous person sins</u>, then <u>he will get punished</u>, **not his generations to come**.

Ezekiel 18:25-32
 God keeps telling them to repent and they will not die. God promises you a new heart and a new spirit. Repentance is the action of turning away from sin and choosing to live in righteousness.

Ezekiel 18:30-32
 "Therefore I will judge you, O house of Israel, each according to his conduct," declares the Lord God. "Repent and turn away from all your transgressions, so that iniquity may not become a stumbling block to you. Cast away from you all your transgressions which you have committed and make yourselves a new heart and a new spirit! For why will you die, O house of Israel? For I have no pleasure in the death of anyone who dies," declares the Lord God. "Therefore, repent and live."

<u>God repeatedly tells **us** to choose life.</u>
- see Proverbs 19:16.

God does not have <u>any</u> pleasure in the death of <u>anyone</u>!

John 9:2-5
"And His disciples asked him, saying, Master, <u>who did sin,</u> this man, or his parents, <u>that he was born blind</u>? Jesus answered, <u>Neither hath this man sinned, nor his parents</u>: but that the works of God should be made manifest in him <u>I must work the</u>

<u>works of Him that sent me</u>, while it is day: the night cometh, when no man can work. <u>As long as I am in the world, I am the light of the world</u>"

If Jesus believed in Generational Curses, this would have been the time to address it. Instead, He ignores the Generational Curse question and points to His own responsibility to set the man free while He is able to, alive on the earth.

2 Corinthians 5:17-21
"Therefore **if anyone** is in **Christ**, *he is* **a new creature***; the **<u>old things passed away</u>**; behold, new things have come. Now **all** *these* things are from God, who reconciled us to Himself through Christ and <u>gave us the ministry of reconciliation</u>, namely, that God was in Christ reconciling the world to Himself, not counting their trespasses against them, and He has committed to us the word of reconciliation. Therefore, we are ambassadors for Christ, as though God were making an appeal through us; we beg you on behalf of Christ, be reconciled to God. He made Him who knew no sin *to be* sin on our behalf, so that we might **become the righteousness of God in Him**."

"new creature" in this text means a new species that never existed before*

You are blessed by God and He has said every good thing He can say about you. He is not cursing you.

Q: What does Galatians 3:13 state?

_____
_____
_____
_____
_____
_____

Where's The <u>Beef</u>?

Jesus taught His disciples the process of growth in order to go from a <u>child</u> to an **adult**. The terminology they used was <u>milk</u> and **meat** or **solid food** of the word.

The <u>milk is the Word of God</u>
The **meat/solid food** is the *action* of *doing* the Word of God.

(Hebrews 5:12-14)
 Those who have become 'dull of hearing' are in need of *milk* once again. Milk is the basic teaching of the Word of God. The Word of God has the power to nourish us, but **if we live *just* off the milk we will *remain children*.**

 Everyone who lives on <u>milk</u> is <u>unskilled</u> in the word of righteousness. **Solid food is for those who have their powers trained by constant practice.** The Hebrew writer says to the Hebrews that they should be teaching, but instead, they have <u>regressed so drastically</u> that they now, <u>once again, needed teaching</u>. With milk alone, not solid food, a child will begin to starve and his growth will slow or even regress. The Hebrews being addressed had not actually understood that you can <u>only</u> grow up into maturity when you begin to *DO* what you have been sent to *DO*. The <u>Milk nourishes and encourages</u>, but the **Meat grows us up into Christ**.

(1 Corinthians 3:1-5)
 Paul calls the Corinthians babes and carnally minded. Envy, strife and division is <u>evidence of carnally minded Christians</u>. <u>Babes</u> and <u>carnally minded believers</u> can <u>only have milk</u>. **Spiritually minded** or **mature believers** can handle **meat**.

(1 Peter 2:1-3)
 The milk (the Word of God) was clearly the prescription for carnality and immaturity in Christ. But just as sure as you need milk you also need meat / solid food. Any child when they are newly born lives purely on their mother's milk, but after a while meat / solid food must be introduced so that the child's growth is not

stunted but encouraged. Similarly, <u>a believer that only lives off milk will stagnate their own spiritual growth</u> if they do not partake in **meat** / solid food.

James 1:22-25
"But prove yourselves **doers of the word**, and not <u>merely hearers</u> who delude themselves. For if anyone is <u>a hearer of the word</u> and <u>not a doer</u>, he is like a man who looks at his natural face in a mirror; for *once* he has looked at himself and gone away, <u>he has immediately forgotten what kind of person he was</u>. But one who looks intently at the perfect law, the *law* of liberty, and **abides by it**, not having become <u>a forgetful hearer</u> but an **effectual doer**, this man will be blessed in what **he does**."

When the <u>milk is received</u> it provides the **encouragement needed to act** in accordance with God's will, but <u>until the Word of God is acted upon</u> it is only a <u>seed waiting to germinate</u>. So the milk is the word of God and the meat / solid food is **to do** <u>the word</u>. This teaching comes from Jesus.

Luke 6:46-49
"Why do you call Me, 'Lord, Lord,' and do not **do** what I **say**? Everyone who comes to Me and **hears My words** and **acts on them**, I will show you whom he is like: he is like a man building a house, who dug deep and laid a **foundation** on the rock; and when a flood occurred, the torrent burst against that house and **could not shake it**, because it had been well built. But the one who <u>has heard</u> and <u>has not acted</u> *accordingly,* is like a man who built a house on the ground <u>without any foundation</u>; and the torrent burst against it and immediately <u>it collapsed, and the ruin of that house was great</u>."

(Matthew 7:24-27)
The ONLY difference Jesus gives between the wise man, and the foolish man is that one **acted on the word he heard**. <u>They both heard the exact same message!</u> The meat of the Word is <u>ONLY</u> gained by putting the Word of God <u>into practice</u>. (Obedience) It is NOT head knowledge. When you are getting your driver's license, you first <u>learn about</u> the laws of driving, but it is not until you get behind the wheel that you actually learn to drive.

(John 4:25-36)
Jesus' disciples return from going to find him food but it doesn't seem like Jesus is hungry. They begin to ask if anyone else brought Him food.
While Jesus's disciples were making arrangements for lunch, He had been sharing the gospel with a Samaritan woman. Jesus then explains that his **meat** or solid food is to **do the will of Him who sent Him** and to finish His Work.

John 4:34
"Jesus saith unto them, My **meat** is to **do** the will of him that sent me, and to finish his work."

(John 6:27-29)
Jesus tells us to **work** for the **meat** that does not perish. When Jesus spoke about **meat**, He was talking about **the works of God**. Meat that endures is not a physical food but one that is eternal life. We are to do **the works of God - Healing the sick**, **casting out demons**, and **setting the captives free**.

The more you DO (eat meat) the gospel, the more you will grow up into Christ.

Q: What does Jesus commission us to do in order to mature?

_____
_____
_____
_____
_____
_____

Jesus In His Own Home Town

A study of the gospels will show that there was <u>not one</u> instance where Jesus ministered to anyone that was sick or a demoniac and they did not get healed or delivered. **Jesus never failed**.

Matthew 4:23-24
"Jesus went throughout Galilee, teaching in their synagogues, preaching the gospel of the kingdom, and **healing every disease and sickness** among the people. News about Him spread all over Syria, and people brought to Him **all who were ill** with various diseases, those suffering acute pain, the demon-possessed, those having seizures, and the paralyzed—**and He healed them**."

Luke 4:40
"At sunset, **all who were ill** with various diseases were brought to Jesus, and <u>laying His hands on each one</u>, **He healed them**."

Jesus healed them ALL

(Mark 6:1-6)
What many believe is that "Jesus *tried* to heal those of His own home town, but He could not heal anyone" which is incorrect! Scripture says: He could there do no mighty works because of their unbelief, <u>except he laid his hands</u> on the sick people **and healed them**.

No one in Nazareth got healed on their own faith, but rather on the faith of Jesus. The unbelief of the people of Nazareth likely kept them from coming to Jesus to be healed. Even under these conditions, **Jesus was able to heal them all**.

So, if Jesus can heal even in His own home town after His own neighbors have become offended at Him, then **SO CAN YOU!**

Looking at the accounts of Jesus going to His own hometown will provide an all encompassing point of view. You can find them in Matthew 13:53-58 and Luke 4:16-30.

 Interesting enough you will see that in the Luke account they were <u>so offended</u> at Jesus <u>they wanted to throw Him off a cliff</u>.

True Fasting & Intercession

Many people are familiar with fasting at least once a year according to the church they belong to. The belief system seems to be that giving up food for a period of time will get gifts from God or cause an "open-heaven."

In Matthew 17:2, the King James Version Bible records Jesus as saying, "[this kind does not go out except by prayer and fasting.]" **Jesus never said that**. When the King James Bible was first printed, it had a note beside that verse saying, "This is not scripture," but the note has been dropped in more recent years, and now it is considered scripture by many who have built a false doctrine around fasting.

Jesus could not have reprimanded His disciples for a lack of fasting, because a few chapters earlier, He told the Pharisees that His disciples could not fast as long as He was with them.

Matthew 9:14-15
"Then the disciples of John came to Him, asking, "Why do we and the Pharisees fast, but Your disciples do not fast?" And Jesus said to them, "The attendants of the bridegroom cannot mourn **as long as the bridegroom is with them**, can they? But the days will come when the bridegroom is taken away from them, and then they will fast."

This is repeated in Mark 2:19-20
"And Jesus said to them, "While the bridegroom is with them, the attendants of the bridegroom cannot fast, can they? **So long as they have the bridegroom with them**, they cannot fast. But the days will come when the bridegroom is taken away from them, and then they will fast in that day."

Q: Is Jesus with you, or not?

_____

_____

God <u>did not</u> like the fast that was done in Israel.
They sought after their own pleasure.

Isaiah 58:2-6
"Yet they seek Me day by day and delight to know My ways, As a nation that has done righteousness And has not forsaken the ordinance of their God. They ask Me *for* just decisions, They delight in the nearness of God. 'Why have we fasted and You do not see? *Why* have we humbled ourselves and You do not notice?' Behold, on the day of your fast you find <u>your</u> <u>desire</u>, And drive hard all your workers. Behold, you fast for contention and strife and to strike with a wicked fist. You do not fast like *you do* today to make your voice heard on high. Is it a fast like this which I choose, a day for a man to humble himself? Is it for bowing one's head like a reed and for spreading out sackcloth and ashes as a bed? <u>Will you call this</u> <u>a fast</u>, even <u>an acceptable day to the Lord</u>? Is this not **the fast which I choose**, **To loosen the bonds of wickedness**, To **undo the bands of the yoke**, And to **let the oppressed go free** And **break every yoke?**"

Isaiah 58:13
"If because of the sabbath, you turn your foot From doing your *own* pleasure on My holy day, And call the sabbath a delight, the holy *day* of the Lord honorable, And honor it, desisting from your *own* ways, From seeking your *own* pleasure **And speaking *your own* word**,"

 Jesus taught fasting in Matthew 6 to the Jews who fasted as part of their traditions and beliefs. Still, He did not practice fasting food with His own disciples, and said that as long as He was with them they WOULD NOT fast food.

 Acts 13:2-3, and 14:23 are the **only** references to fasting found in the New Covenant, and it was only in connection to making decisions on appointing people to leadership.
 2 Corinthians 11:27 is talking about Paul being forced to go without food and water, not fasting by choice
 Acts 27:9 was talking about "The fast." (The day of atonement) which was a season known for bad weather on the seas. It is making a point.

There are four additional references where King James added fasting into his Bible because HE WANTED IT, but **it was not scripture.**

Many religious traditions were still falling away in the early church. Jesus is our example. He only fasted ONCE at the beginning of His ministry when He was tempted FOR US, fulfilling the law. After that, it says that the generation called Jesus a glutton because of His eating. (Matthew 11:19)

(Isaiah 58:12)

God is already on your side in Heaven. You do not need to get Him to help you through, "fasting and intercession." In fact, Jesus is already interceding FOR you in Heaven right now! And He is waiting on YOU to respond to His commands, trusting that His Word is true.

How Much Faith Do I Need?

The word 'faith' has been over-spiritualised through the years to the degree that it has almost lost all of its original meaning. Faith is often thought of as a heavenly currency one uses to get things from God. Many falsely believe that they need to do something more to gain enough faith for God to work in their lives.

(Hebrews 11:1-3)
Faith is the confidence of things hoped for and the conviction of things not seen. Faith is simply the conviction that the one who made the promise is faithful to keep his word.

(Romans 10:17)
Faith <u>comes by hearing</u> the word of God. Listen to the word of God on audio, read it outloud, or discuss it with others to receive the best results.

Do not allow the enemy to speak his lies to you, replace the lies with the Truth of the Word of God.

(2 Corinthians 5:7)
We walk by faith, not by sight in the carnal realm.

The Three forms of Faith

1. Faith for Yourself.
In Mark 5:25-34 the woman chose when she was getting healed. She chose *how* she was getting healed. <u>She had faith for herself</u>.

2. Faith for Someone Else.
In Mark 3:1-6 the man with a withered hand did not have faith for himself. <u>Jesus had faith for that man</u>. Jesus was surrounded by people who were against him. **Jesus did not let any negative circumstances stop him.**

3. Third Party Faith.
(Mark 2:4-12) It was the paralytic's friends who brought him to Jesus. They had determination to get the paralytic to Jesus. Jesus saw the faith of the friends.

Either the person had faith for themselves, or for another person, or Jesus had faith for them. You will not do well if you think you must rely on someone else's faith for their healing. You do not need anyone's faith but your own for the power of Jesus to set someone free. Otherwise, how would you ever raise the dead?

In order for healing to work, only one person needs to act in faith.

Q: What is Faith?

_____

_____

_____

_____

_____

_____

If we compare the two stories where Jesus commends people for their great faith, notice that <u>none of these people were in direct covenant with God.</u> None of them were Jews! It takes greater faith to receive the benefits from a position that you do not hold.

Matthew 8:5-13
The Roman Centurion understood authority because he used authority in <u>the same way Jesus demonstrated it</u>. Jesus commended the Roman Centurion for his <u>great faith</u>. In another version of the Bible, we learn that Jesus was not speaking to the Roman Centurion but rather to a messenger. (Luke 7:1-10)
This is a good example of third party faith where the Roman Centurion had faith on behalf of someone else.

(Matthew 15:21-28)
 The Canaanite woman came to Jesus to ask for help for her daughter. Jesus first tells her no. This is the only time Jesus says no. The Canaanite woman did not take no for an answer. Jesus gave her what she wanted, and her daughter was healed. Jesus commends her for her <u>great faith</u>.

Faith always gets what it comes for.

 The disciples witnessed that Jesus commended the Roman Centurion and the Canaanite woman for their <u>great faith</u>. They thought that they would need to increase their faith as well.

(Luke 17:5-6)
 The disciples asked Jesus to help them increase their faith. Jesus answered them by telling them that they only need faith like a grain of a mustard seed. If they **only believed** they could move mountains.

Some Christians believe you need a bigger mustard seed
before you speak to the mountain.
You do not need <u>great faith</u>.
Just faith.

The Truth About The Anointing

We have been taught that there are only certain people who are anointed, such as church leaders. It is a false belief that special anointings must be imparted from the laying on of hands if we want to do anything big for God.

"Anointed" Definition:
(Chrio) To smear or rub with oil, that is, (by implication) to consecrate to an office or religious service: - anoint.

(Exodus 40:9-15)
In the Old Covenant, anointing was about putting something aside to be used in a specific task. i.e. The things that were only to be used in the tabernacle were anointed.
Aaron and his sons were anointed for the purpose of serving as priests.
The oil and the pouring of it over Aaron, his sons and the equipment was an outward symbol of their appointment to office.

 God anointed the Prophets to be His voice on the Earth in the Old Testament.
Like Moses, the prophets acted as a mediator between God and the people.

(Exodus 30:30)
The purpose of Aaron's and his sons' anointing was that their office of priest was to be passed down from generation to generation. They were consecrated 'to perform a function'.

In order to accomplish His will on the earth God appointed prophets, priests, and kings in His stead. Looking at Jesus' life, you will see that Jesus was *all* of these things.

We are anointed just as Jesus!
This makes us prophets, priests, and kings!

(Luke 4:16-19)
Jesus was reading out of the scroll of the Prophet, Isaiah.
He has been <u>anointed to</u>:
Proclaim good news to the poor
Proclaim liberty to the captives
Recovering the sight to the blind.
To set at liberty those who are oppressed
To proclaim the year of the Lord's favor.

(Acts 10:38)
Jesus was <u>anointed</u> when the <u>Holy Spirit came upon Him</u>. (Anointed) At that point <u>He received power</u> to heal all who were oppressed by the devil.

Acts 1:8
A Believer will receive power once the Holy Spirit has come upon them. (Anointed) Then, they are all called to go into all the earth and heal all who are oppressed by the devil.

God has anointed us with *the same anointing as* Jesus!
There is no better anointing in the New Covenant.

1 John 2:27
"As for you, the anointing which you received <u>from Him</u> <u>abides in you</u>, and you have no need for anyone to teach you; but as His anointing teaches you about all things, and is true and is not a lie, and just as it has taught you, you abide in Him."

God has chosen to gift us with His Holy Spirit.
We do not need to be anointed by anyone else.
We have ALL the anointing and power needed to do the works that Jesus did and greater.

Q: How does a Believer in Jesus receive His anointing?

_____

_____

_____

_____

_____

_____

Pool of Bethesda

Many people believe that Jesus only healed one person at the pool of Bethesda. Many false teachings have come from this assumption, such as the belief that the Holy Spirit led Jesus to not heal anybody else and that God chooses who He heals and who He does not. But is this really what this particular story is telling us?

This is **one** testimony of **one** healing of **one** guy at **one** time.

(John 5:1-16)
John was the only person to record this instance of healing that Jesus did. There is no record that says Jesus did or did not heal others at Bethesda specifically.

Acts 10:38 says Jesus healed ALL

It is very interesting that the same book that recorded the healing about Bethesda is also the same book that states that if everything that Jesus did was written down, the whole world would not contain all the books.
(John 21:25)

Knowing the nature of Jesus He would have healed more at the pool of Bethesda rather than only healing one and leaving the others.

Q: What other scriptures show us that Jesus healed them all?

_____
_____
_____
_____

Rhema vs. Logos

 Traditionally we have been taught that Logos is the written Word in the Bible, and Rhema is the spoken Word. The belief is that if a scripture meant something to you, or you got a divine revelation or a leading, then you got a Rhema Word. Do we need a Rhema word from God before we can act on a scripture?

Strong's Concordance for Logos, and Rhema:

Logos: <u>something said or thought</u>, a topic or subject of discourse, also reasoning or motive; an account, cause, communication, preaching, question, speaker, speech, talk, thing, utterance, word, work.

Rhema: <u>an utterance</u> (individually, collectively or specifically); by implication, a matter or topic (especially of narration, command or dispute)

Verse	Text	Greek Word
John 1:1	In the beginning was the **Word**, and the **Word** was with God, and the **Word** was God.	Logos
John 1:14	The **Word** became flesh and made his dwelling among us. We have seen his glory, the glory of the one and only Son, who came from the Father, full of grace and truth.	Logos
John 4:37	Thus the **saying** 'One sows and another reaps' is true.	Logos
John 5:47	But since you do not believe what he wrote, how are you going to believe what I **say**?	Rhema
John 6:60	On hearing it, many of his disciples said,, "This is a hard **teaching**. Who can accept it?"	Logos
John 6:63	The Spirit gives life; the flesh counts for nothing. The **words** that I have spoken to you - they are full of the Spirit and life.	Rhema

 You have just looked at a few verses where Logos and Rhema are used in John and Ephesians. There is practically no difference between the two words in the

Strong's Concordance Dictionary, and in the use of the words. They are used **interchangeably** in scripture.

Instead of getting caught up in Greek synonyms, let's look at **what Jesus said about His words**.

Matthew 7:24-27

"Therefore everyone <u>who hears these words</u> of Mine **and acts on them** is like a **wise** man who built his house on the rock. The rain fell, the torrents raged, and the winds blew and beat against that house; yet it did not fall, because its foundation was on the **rock**.

But everyone who hears these words of Mine **and <u>does not</u>** act on them is like a **foolish** man who built his house on **sand**. The rain fell, the torrents raged, and the winds blew and beat against that house, and it fell—and great was its collapse!"

What was the difference that <u>mattered to Jesus</u>? Everyone who hears His words and **acts on them** them is **wise**. Nothing can stand against those who **do** the words of Jesus. Those who <u>hear</u> the words of Jesus and <u>do *not* do them</u>, are <u>fools</u>. Let's focus on what matters to Him.

<u>Great is the fall</u> of the ones who <u>do not act</u> on the command of Jesus.

Logos <u>OR</u> Rhema, those who <u>act</u> on the words of Jesus are wise, and stable.

Q: What is the difference between the wise man and the foolish man?

_____

_____

_____

_____

The Chastisement Of God

There has been an underlying belief within the body of Christ that trials and problems as well as sicknesses have been designed by God to make you stronger. For instance, it has been said that "God led the children of Israel into the wilderness to make their faith stronger." Did the wilderness really make their faith stronger, or did it kill them? <u>They never even saw the promised land</u>.
It was <u>because</u> of **their disobedience** that they had spent forty years in the wilderness, **not God's doing**.

(Hebrews 4:1-3)
The Isrealites <u>did not unite **faith** with **God's word**</u>. God had *told them* that the promised land was <u>theirs</u> and **they were** to **possess it**, but they did not. It was their disobedience and lack of trust in God's Word that kept them from the promised land.

Hebrews 11:6
"And without faith it is impossible to please Him, for he who comes to God must believe that He is and that He is a rewarder of those who seek Him."

God is for us, He does not teach us things by giving us sickness and trials.

When <u>any</u> situation comes your way, and *you* act <u>according to God's word</u>, He will cause you to come out of that situation stronger. However, tribulations are NOT from God.

God is **NEVER** the giver of calamity, sorrows or sickness.

(Proverbs 10:22)
The Blessing of the Lord makes us rich. It adds <u>no sorrow</u> with it. <u>Calamity is *not* a blessing</u>. <u>Poverty is *not* a blessing</u>. <u>Sickness is *not* a blessing</u>. If sorrow comes with something, then it is not from our heavenly Father!

(James 1:17)
God is our Father, and He gives us good gifts. Sickness is not a good gift, problems are not good gifts. These don't come from God.

(Mark 4:17)
Trials and persecution are not designed by God to make you stronger. Jesus says that <u>they have been designed by the devil</u> **to STEAL the Word**!

Persecution arises on account of the Word.

James 4:17
"<u>Submit</u> therefore <u>to God</u>. <u>Resist the devil</u> and he will flee from you."

If everything that happened to you was from God, Why would His Word direct you to resist the devil?

Not everything that happens to you is God's will. There is a chastening of the Lord, but <u>it is **always** good</u>.

You need to see that the word <u>chasten</u> is <u>to child train</u>, **not abuse**.

(Hebrews 12:5-7)
God addresses (speaks) to us as sons. A <u>good father</u> would <u>train and discipline</u> his child. The scriptures are *not* saying that God is sending some calamity your way to teach you. <u>That would be child abuse</u> not child training.

Q: How does a Believer 'resist the devil'?

_____

_____

_____

_____

God could *not* use sickness to train His children unless He stole it first as sickness does not come from Heaven! There is no sickness in Heaven!

Matthew 7:9-11
"Or what man is there among you who, when his son asks for a loaf, will give him a stone? Or if he asks for a fish, he will not give him a snake, will he? If you then, being evil, know how to give good gifts to your children, how much more will your Father who is in heaven give what is good to those who ask Him!"

You wouldn't have a disease brought upon your own kids because you know it's wrong, and neither would God.

God is the best Father that the world has ever known, and He ONLY gives good gifts.

2 Timothy 3:16-17
"All Scripture is inspired by God and profitable for teaching, for reproof, for correction, for training in righteousness; so that the man of God may be adequate, equipped for every good work."

The word of God is what God uses to correct His children. (John 14:26)
He convicts people of wrong by His Word through the inward witness of His spirit. The Holy Spirit in you desires to walk as Jesus, and to stop anything that is *not of God*. That "nails on the chalk-board" inside you when something is wrong, is the Holy Spirit nudging you that what is going on is not of Him.

God also chastises through mature believers in the body of Christ which can be in the form of prophecy, or a direct confrontation. (James 5:19-20, 1 Corinthians)

The purpose is always to bring them to repentance so that they are restored.

The Purpose Of The Gift Of The Spirit

The Holy Spirit *is* the gift through which all the 'parts of the Spirit' flow.

1 Corinthians describes these parts of the Spirit as; Word of wisdom, word of knowledge, faith, gifts of healings, working of miracles, prophecy, discerning of spirits, different kinds of tongues, interpretation of tongues
Isaiah describes them as; The Spirit of The Lord (Jehovah), the Spirit of wisdom and understanding, counsel and strength, knowledge and the fear of the Lord.
Romans 12 describes them as: Prophecy, Serving, Teaching, Exhortation, Giving, Leadership, Mercy

Sons of God *have THE gift* of The Holy Spirit and can choose to operate in any manifestation of The Holy Spirit at any time.

When you operate in the authority provided for you by Jesus, **all** aspects of the Holy Spirit follow.
Jesus Christ never had to operate in a gift.
The fullness of Christ operates in Authority & Dominion.

(1 Corinthians 12:22-31)
Paul urged the Corinthians to earnestly desire the higher gifts. He was not teaching that we were limited to whichever gifts you were given. We may not see Believers operating in the fullness of the Spirit however scripture shows us we must earnestly desire to do so.

Immediately after Paul lists out the gifts in 1 Corinthians 12, he says, "but I show you a better way." The better way is Jesus.

Q: Why does Paul say there is a better way than operating in the 'gifts of the Holy Spirit'?

_____

_____

_____

_____

_____

The Holy Spirit has <u>empowered us</u> **to do** the will of the Father and He teaches us to discern what is of Him and **cooperate** with Him in order to operate in the full power of Jesus Christ. When we simply believe, and release the Kingdom, whatever manifestation is needed will be given to the person or people in front of us.

Q: How does the Holy Spirit equip Believers to *do* the Word of God?

_____

_____

_____

(Ephesians 4:11-16)
The aim of the four fold ministry (internal leadership; Pastor-Teacher, Prophet, Apostle, Evangelist) for the body of Christ is that we **all grow up into the fullness of Christ in every way**. When we are mature we will <u>no longer be tossed to and fro by every wind of doctrine</u>. We will speak the truth, and build the whole body up in love.

(1 Corinthians 12:1-6)
There are varieties of gifts, but <u>the same Spirit</u>.
There are varieties of services, but <u>the same Lord</u>.
There are varieties of activities, but <u>the same God</u>.
<u>It is the **same** Jesus that empowers **all** Believers.</u>

The fruits that are evidenced when a believer is walking by the Spirit; are Love, Joy, Peace, Patience, Kindness, Goodness, Faithfulness, Gentleness, Self-Control (Galatians 5:22-23)

If you're a Believer, there isn't any part of Jesus that you didn't get. Asking which gift of the Spirit you got is like asking which fruit of the Spirit you got. You have the ability to function in it all!

All can do All.

You will know the true Spirit of God by the fruit of His power demonstrated in and through you.

Jesus never made a decision based on carnal influence; the eyes and the ears of the carnal senses, or the fear of man. He knew the Spirit of God.

(Isaiah 11)
"He will not judge by what His eyes see, Nor make a decision by what His ears hear"
Jesus knew what was right. From childhood, He had learned the Father's will, and acted on it. God remains the same, yesterday, today and He will never change. God functions in an attitude of full righteousness, judgment, and authority, always resulting in repentance.

Through Sons of God (YOU!), the Spirit of God will make all enemies His footstool, and the world will function in the beauty that it was created to.

The Power Of Your Words

What we speak carries power. It will have either a positive or a negative consequence in our lives.

Proverbs 18:21
"Death and life are in the power of the tongue,
And those who love it will eat its fruit."

Whatever circumstance you face, *you have the* **choice** to speak life or death over it. **What we say will bear fruit**.

Q: What fruits of the Spirit do words of life bare?

_____

_____

_____

_____

_____

_____

Q: Give examples of speaking life versus death.

_____

_____

_____

_____

_____

_____

_____

_____

_____

(James 3:3-5)
 Horses and ships are directed by very small things. Cars have a steering wheel, which is small compared to the rest of the car, yet without it, you cannot steer the car in any direction you need to go. Our tongue and the words it produces **directs our lives and our health** and **the well being of others**.

(James 3:9-12)
 As Believers, our words should be uplifting and bringing forth LIFE reflecting our faith in God's Word. Words of death should never roll off our tongues.
 We are to speak, and act like Jesus in all ways.

> Our words are powerful seeds that have
> the power to build up or destroy lives.

 Audibly speaking out God's Word is a powerful weapon which strengthens our faith. It will also redirect our situation to God's will.
 Romans 10:17 says that faith comes by hearing. So, make sure that YOU can hear yourself read and declare God's truth. Do not simply read silently in your head.

(Ephesians 6:17)
> The word of God is the sword of the Spirit. It is a powerful weapon which is effective for everyday use against the enemy.

 To personalize the Word of God, take a New Covenant scripture, and change the wording to relate to you and your situation, without changing the truth. Use the present tense, and past tense. (The work has already been done by Jesus) Have the mindset that it is finished.

 Romans 8:2 could be personalized to say, "I have been set free from all in the law of sin and death by the law of the spirit of LIFE in Christ Jesus."

 2 Corinthians 5:17 could be personalized to say, "Because I am in Christ, I am a New Creation. The old things are gone, and now ALL things in me are new!"

Remember that any verse such as these can also be used to speak over _others_. The Word of God is always the plumb line of prophecy. You can encourage others powerfully with this tool. Just pick any New Covenant scripture about identity in Christ to begin speaking truth over their lives.

Romans 8:2 could be prophetically declared over someone to say, "_Sally_ has been set free from ALL sin and death because _she_ has been filled with the spirit of LIFE. Jesus lives in _her_!"

2 Corinthians 5:17 could be prophetically declared over someone to say, "Friend, YOU are in Christ. That means that you are a new creation. All of your past, and your old life is gone. Right now, all things in you are new, and perfect. That is what God says about you."

Q: Give additional examples of personalizing scripture to speak over yourself and the lives of your loved ones.

_____

_____

_____

_____

_____

_____

Continue to speak the Word of God, and **only** those things which give LIFE by the anointing of God. Do not change your confession to negative words. It is better to talk less, or be silent than to spend time agreeing with satan by your words.

Boldly confess the Scriptures over your life daily. The next page is an example of a biblical Believer's vocabulary to get you started.

I believe God's Word. I can do what it says I can. I believe what it tells me about who I am. I acknowledge every good thing that is in me, that is also in Christ Jesus, who lives in and through me. It is not I who live, but Christ who lives in me. I died, was buried, and was raised up with Him. I sit in heavenly places far above all principalities and powers, even sickness and diseases. I command sickness to GO! And it FLEES! I tell poverty to GO! And it GOES! God has given me the ability to create wealth so that I establish His Kingdom on the Earth.

I'm healthy, strong and an overcomer, because greater is He that is in me than he that is in the world. I tread upon serpents and scorpions, and nothing shall by any means hurt me. Nothing will touch my family or come near my household. I have authority over all the abilities of the enemy. Every weapon the enemy attempts to form against me will not prosper. I do not have fear, but I have the Spirit of power, love and a sound mind. I am patient, I am kind, I don't rejoice in evil doing. I am not irritated nor am I envious. I don't look for love. I am love. I have clarity of thought because I keep my mind on Jesus and He is praiseworthy. I stay in perfect peace. The Law of the Spirit of life has set me free from the law of sin and death. I am free from sin. Sin no longer has dominion over me because I walk in holiness, not in sin. I walk in His righteousness, I walk in life, not sickness nor death. I have life abundant! I have enough life to give away. I have life, I have health, I have wisdom, I have strength, I have wealth. I have love. I am a life giving spirit that flows constantly into eternity, I am blessed with every spiritual gift which is from heaven. Jesus is Lord over me, and over my house. He is Lord of my health, and finances, Lord over my family and my property. Everything I own belongs to Him, and therefore the devil can't touch it. Jesus is KING!

The anointing that is in me does not come and go. Where I go, it goes. The Father, Jesus, and the Holy Spirit dwell in me. I am so full of God there is no room for anything else. I am full of life. I am the highest spiritual authority wherever I go. When people get around me they get infected with life. They get healed. I will make disciples of every nation, showing them that the gospel is the Power of God unto salvation. I will not use persuasive words, but I will use the power of demonstration so that their faith would rest on the power of God. I do the same works that Jesus did and greater because He went to the Father. My light shines so that all men can see my good works and give glory to Him.

Amen!

The ABCD Of Ministry (Jesus Style)

A. Availability
To be available, someone has to have access to you, and you have to be available for them. Jesus never put off anyone due to it being inconvenient and neither should we.

Q: Give examples of making yourself accessible and available.

_____

_____

_____

_____

B. Boldness
One of the primary signs that a Believer was filled with the Holy Spirit of Jesus, was that they spoke with holy **boldness**. Jesus had holy boldness.
(Acts 4:13, 31) (Acts 14:3)

Holy boldness always <u>speaks on behalf of God</u>. Carnal chattiness is not boldness.

Never let any fear control how you minister

C. Compassion
Many people think that compassion is a form of empathy or a form of sympathy. <u>It is neither of these two things.</u>
Empathy is where you are some-what sympathetic towards the person's situation. You associate with it, and you understand where they are at so you try to make them realize that you do understand.
Sympathy looks on the situation and says, "Oh it's horrible that you're there, but that is what your lot in life is."
Compassion is different. It is when you look at a situation and something rises up inside of you and **demands that the situation must change because** it is not of

God, and it should not continue any more. <u>It is a drive on the inside of you</u> to defend the innocent, weak or oppressed. **Compassion is never *emotion*.** You are influenced by compassion when you see someone bully a kid, and when you see someone say something to someone that they should never have said because it was wrong. That drive inside of you is compassion, this is what drove Jesus.

How many scriptures tell you to be led by emotions? None. Stay out of emotions!

Compassion is a drive to action, and you must have it to be effective in ministry.

(Matthew 9:35-10:11)
When Jesus saw the multitudes in great need, He ordained His disciples and gave them authority over devils to drive them out, and to heal the sick. The whole reason Jesus appointed His disciples was because of compassion; He <u>saw the need</u> and <u>acted on it.</u> He did not ordain the disciples because they had gone through a seminary college.

Jesus appointed the disciples <u>because He saw the need and knew that the disciples knew Truth</u>. Jesus did NOT appoint the disciples based on their own abilities.

**Compassion is frequently mentioned throughout scripture.
Jesus' miracles were motivated by compassion.**

- Jesus healed the sick because of compassion - Matt 14:14
- Jesus healed the blind man because of compassion - Matt 20:29-34
- Jesus healed the leper because of compassion - Mark 1:40
- Jesus cast out devils because of compassion - Mark 5:18-19
- Jesus fed the multitude because of compassion - Matt 15:32
- Jesus raised the dead because of compassion - Luke 7:11-16

Whenever Jesus had compassion something miraculous happened. His love stirred up aggression towards the things that would rob someone of the fullness of the life God wanted them to have. It was at the whipping post and on the cross where Jesus destroyed the works of the devil once and for all. Now, we are motivated by compassion because the love of God compels us to act on behalf of those who are illegally being oppressed.

D. Determination
You have heard the statement that often 'the difference between failure and success is your willingness to persevere.' This saying is so true. One thing we have lost in our super drive-through generation is the fact that you need to persevere, and be determined. These days, if people try a sport without immediate success, they quit. Then, they want to watch the movies about the underdog that is so determined, he actually succeeds. **Determination is a learned quality**. Learn to be determined, so that YOU will have your own testimonies, and fruit to show for Jesus, instead of only hearing about everyone else's.

Paul said in Hebrews 12 to run the race with *patience* to win. That word means to **actively, diligently pursue the promise until you get it.**
This is how we should be as we are ministering.

Determination is the quality of being determined. It is a firmness of purpose.

Galatians 6:9
"Let us not grow weary in well-doing, for in due season we will <u>reap a harvest</u> if we do not give up."

Your Determination influences the outcome

A careful study of the gospels will show that there was not one instance where Jesus ministered to anyone that was sick, or a demoniac that did not get healed or delivered. Jesus never failed, and He is our example.

(Matthew 4:23-24)
Jesus healed them ALL

(Luke 4:40-44)
Jesus laid His hands on the sick and everyone got healed.

Very often when you are getting a sick person healed, they will inevitably give you a whole history lesson about how this illness came upon them. The reality is that we do not need to know every detail. It would be wise to stop them from talking about the sickness, and just get them healed like Jesus did.

Jesus did not require a diagnosis in order to set someone free.

(Mark 10:51-52)
At times Jesus asked what they needed and granted it to them. That was enough to get the job done.

(Matthew 9:20-22)
Sometimes the sick simply touched Jesus to be healed. Jesus did not need to know anything about the sickness in order to know that whatever it was, it had to go.

Jesus would heal with a command or touch.
We should do the same.

How To Minister Healing / Deliverance

<u>Do not talk to God</u> about the problem.
Tell the problem to "GO!"

Do **not** pray long prayers as the Pharisees.

Jesus never spoke more than one sentence
for a person's healing or deliverance.

Less words. More power.

Identify measurable symptoms or what the person is unable to do.

1. <u>Attack:</u> Command the enemy. Lay hands where possible.
2. <u>Check:</u> Ask the person to check for changes. If needed, repeat 1 & 2.
3. <u>Praise:</u> Give thanks to Jesus and testify of what happened.

Examples:
1.) "Are you in pain or have any measurable symptoms?"
        "Yes."
"Where would you rate your pain? 0 being no pain and 10 the worst ever."
"Do you want it to go?"
        "Yes."
(Then reach out to grab their hand or lay your hand on them and command the devil, "GO!")
"Now, do what you couldn't do before" / "Check it."

Or you could ask

2.) "May I speak a blessing over you?"
"In the name of Jesus, and the power of the Holy Spirit, I speak LIFE!"

Or

3.) "If you could have one miracle from God today, what would it be?"
(Then lay your hand on their shoulder, declare -speak out- their miracle and believe)

Q: Give an example of speaking out - declaring for somebody's miracle.

_____

_____

_____

_____

_____

_____

_____

_____

_____

_____

Dealing With Failure

The only true failure is failing to <u>obey</u> God.

Jesus summed up every reason for failure in **one word** the first time His disciples didn't get someone free; unbelief.

Matthew 17:19-20
"Then came the disciples to Jesus apart, and said, <u>Why could not we cast him out?</u> And Jesus said unto them, <u>Because of your **unbelief**</u>: for verily I say unto you, If ye have faith as a grain of mustard seed, <u>ye shall **say**</u> unto this mountain, Remove hence to yonder place; and it shall remove; and nothing shall be impossible unto you."

Jesus' twelve disciples had been operating in authority, but they pulled back instead of standing on what Jesus had commanded them. Because of their unbelief, (double-mindedness) they could not get the demonized boy free.
This is also a lesson in the will of God. Even when the disciples didn't get the job done, Jesus didn't say, "Oh well, if it was really God's will, the boy would have been cured already. The boy is surely in a season of waiting on My Father's perfect timing." That would be ridiculous! Once Jesus came near, He enforced God's will, rebuked the devil, and the boy was instantly cured.

Unbelief can result because of "**Traditions of men**," which Jesus says will actually nullify the word of God. (Mark 7:13)

Traditions of men are religious attempts to walk in the spirit with no power. It is doing anything outside of the way Jesus showed us to do it, including going back under the Old Covenant.

James says "**Double-Mindedness**" (A form of **unbelief**) causes a person to be unable to *receive* anything from the Lord. This does not mean that He hasn't *already* given it to you!
(James 1:5-8)

Double-Mindedness looks like an unstable decision, "Well, I don't know. I believe, but is God going to heal me, or not?" is a statement of double-mindedness, and unbelief.

Either you know God's will, and you believe His Word, or you don't.

When *we believe*, we *will receive* the promise,
and no longer be tossed to and fro
with every wind of doctrine.

The Old Covenant
The Law, History, Poetry, Prophet, & Gospel Books:

5 Law:	5 Poetry:	Prophets:	4 Gospels:
Genesis	Job	5 Major:	Matthew
Exodus	Psalms	Isaiah	Mark
Leviticus	Proverbs	Jeremiah	Luke
Numbers	Ecclesiastes	Lamentations	John
Deuteronomy	Song of Songs	Ezekiel	
		Daniel	*(This is the time period <u>during the Old Covenant</u> when Jesus was born and raised! Most of the time He was addressing Jews.)*
12 History:		12 Minor:	
Joshua		Hosea	
Judges		Joel	
Ruth		Amos	
1 Samuel		Obediah	
2 Samuel		Jonah	
1 Kings		Micah	
2 Kings		Nahum	
1 Chronicles		Habakkuk	
2 Chronicles		Zephaniah	
Ezra		Haggai	
Nehemiah		Zachariah	
Ester		Malachi	

All of these books were written about people in the <u>Old Covenant</u>.

None of them were in the New Covenant,
until Jesus had finished His work on the cross.
(not even during "the 4 Gospels")

During that time Believers could not ACT in the New Covenant
until The Holy Spirit was poured out on ALL flesh,
on the day of Pentecost, 50 days later!

The Book of **Acts** is the <u>first</u> book of the New Covenant in "The New Testament" **NOW! "It Is Finished!"**

Acts is the testimony of the first generation of New Testament saints, discovering the <u>New Creation life</u> as <u>The Holy Spirit of Christ taught them all things.</u>

Remember
We should be grown up even more fully
as Sons of God that look like Christ than the first generation from the book of Acts.

The Epistles (Letters) Of The New Covenant

Paul to Churches:	Paul to Friends:	General Letters:
Romans	1 Timothy	Hebrews
1 Corinthians	2 Timothy	James
2 Corinthians	Titus	1 Peter
Galatians	Philemon	2 Peter
Ephesians		1 John
Philippians		2 John
Colossians		3 John
1 Thessalonians		Jude
2 Thessalonians		

Each of these books were <u>written by men</u> inspired by the Holy Spirit to *specific people* for a *specific purpose*.

The book of the **Revelation of Jesus Christ** is the last book in what we call the canon written "Bible."

It is an account of the prophetic vision of John, **primarily revealing the glory of Jesus Christ**, and foretelling of the end of time.

The Word of God is **Jesus.** (John 1)
Moses is <u>not</u> The Word of God. (2 Corinthians 3)

The Old Covenant was not written to you, unless you're at least 2,000 years old and born a Jew.
Now, not all of the written "New Testament" applies to you.
It's time to grow up as Sons of God.

Jesus said that we would do greater works, so we have to at least start with the example of Jesus, and learn from principles in the New Covenant that apply to **Sons.**

Examples Of Spiritual Maturity By New Testament Letters

Letter	Maturity	Address	Notes
1 Corinthians	Carnal Baby	vs. 3, 13:11	Very immature, most reprimanded group
2 Corinthians	Child	vs. 6:13; 12:14	They had grown a bit from letter #1
Galatians	Baby	vs. 3:1	Went *back* under the curse of the law
Ephesians	**Son**	vs. 4:14	Most mature group written to in the Bible
Philippians	Child	vs. 2:15	
Colossians	**Son**	context	Very similar to Ephesians
Hebrews	Baby	vs. 5:12-13	
James	Baby	vs. 5:14	A first book written to new Believers

"The problem is that believers don't know if they should be an Old Covenant slave, or a carnal Corinthian who was not spiritual, or like the people in 2 Corinthians where they were tossed to and fro with every wind of doctrine. When you're fully grown you know the will of your Father. You know you should be healed, delivered and born again. You know you should be like Christ in all ways in season and out."

- Dave Lage

Spiritual Babies / Slaves

There are different Greek words used in the Original language to communicate the spiritual maturity of Believers. Not every time you read the word, "child," in the English Bible does it mean the same thing in the original language.
Hebrews and 1 Corinthians are called *both babies and children* in the same letters. They were not behaving as mature Sons of God.

Spiritual Babies are not able to take solid food. They are milk drinkers. Spiritual Babies are fleshly, full of strife and jealousy. They are not spiritual, and act as "mere mortal men." Spiritual Babies are <u>not able to discern</u> anything. They are tossed about by every wind of doctrine. Spiritual Babies <u>wait to be told what to do every day</u>.

(1 Corinthians 3:1-4) (Hebrews 5:11-14) (Ephesians 4:14)

We are <u>not</u> to be spiritual <u>babies</u>, or even <u>children</u> of God. Those who are living as anything less than a **mature Son of God** are double-minded, and unstable in everything they do.

See Where's The Beef Chapter*

The words you **speak** reflect
the spiritual level of your life.

Manifesting Mature Sons Of God

"Perfect," is the attainment of the end or ideal completeness of being. In order to know what a spiritually perfect Son looks like, we only need to look at Jesus in His fullness as He is now.

First of all, we <u>are</u> **commanded** to be perfect in all our ways.
That means we **Can** walk as perfect Sons.
We can do <u>ALL</u> things.

Matthew 5:48
"Therefore <u>you are to be</u> **perfect**, <u>as your heavenly Father</u> is perfect."

Ephesians 4:13
"Until we all attain the unity of the faith, and of the knowledge of the Son of God, to a <u>mature</u> man, to **the measure of the stature which belongs to <u>the fullness of Christ</u>**."

James 3:2
"For we all stumble in many *ways.* If anyone does not stumble **in what he says**, he is a perfect (mature) man, able to bridle the whole body as well."

The book of James was written to new Believers, (not mature) but notice that "**what he says**" will <u>cause</u> a man to either be a <u>baby</u>, or a <u>perfect</u> (complete) Son.

True humility is not thinking less of yourself,
but thinking of yourself less.

Humility is agreeing with God by choosing to see Jesus in
His fullness when you look in the mirror.
It **is being Jesus** to every person around you
<u>because you know who you are</u>.
That is Sonship - Being Jesus to the world every day.

No matter your physical age, anyone can and should be a Mature Son of God.

Jesus is our example. We can do the same works as He did, and greater because we don't look at him in His suffering anymore. He went to the Father and is **now** in the **New Covenant** with us!

A Mature Son of God is:

- A Doer. Jesus acted on the Word. He didn't just talk about it (John 14:31)
- Untouchable. No harm could come to Him until He allowed it (John 10:18)
- Moved by Compassion (Matthew 9:36)
- Anointed by The Holy Ghost (Luke 3:22)
- Healer of ALL who are oppressed by the devil (Acts 10:38)
- Corrects, does not enable people going in wrong directions (Matthew 21:12)
- Does not back down from the enemy (Luke 4:12)
- Does not get caught up in religious tricks (Matthew 21:24)
- Speaks with absolutes (John 6:38)
- Recognized by Hell. Master over the devil (Mark 5:7)
- Glorified by God (Matthew 3:17)

More Qualities of a Mature Son:

Their spiritual senses are trained to **know** when something is from Heaven or Hell, and they <u>know</u> they have the right to <u>judge</u> that difference. (<u>Discernment</u>) (Hebrews 5:14)

They will accurately handle the Word instead of twisting it to make excuses. (2 Timothy 2:15)

This is how **YOU** are commanded to live. <u>*Just*</u> <u>like</u> Jesus.

5 Tips To Success

Discover your <u>Sonship</u>
Assume your Authority
Use your Power
Assess your Wealth
Believe in your Destiny
-T.L. Osborn

29 Differences Between

The Old Covenant (Genesis-Acts Chapter 1) &

The New Covenant (Acts 2-Revelation)

1. John 1:17 - The Old Covenant came through Moses,
The New Covenant came through Jesus Christ.

2. 2 Corinthians 3:6 - The Old Covenant leads to death,
The New Covenant gives life.

3. Romans 10:4 - The Old Covenant was fulfilled by Jesus Christ,
Hebrews 8:6 - **The New Covenant was established by Jesus Christ.**

4. Galatians 5:1 - The Old Covenant enslaves,
John 8:32. 36 - **The New Covenant gives freedom to mankind.**

5. Hebrews 7:19 - The Old Covenant leaves man imperfect,
The New Covenant leaves man perfect.

6. Galatians 3:19 - The Old Covenant exposes sin,
Romans 4:1-8 - **The New Covenant destroys sin.**

7. 2 Corinthians 3:7 - The Old Covenant cannot give life,
Galatians 3:11, 6:8 - **The New Covenant gives life.**

8. Ephesians:2:15 - The Old Covenant was abolished,
The New Covenant is in force.

9. Galatians 3:10 - The Old Covenant brings a curse,
Galatians 3:13 - **The New Covenant redeems from curse.**

10. Galatians 3:10-11 - In the Old Covenant living is by works,
The New Covenant is living by faith.

11. Colossians 2:14-17 - The Old Covenant is a shadow,
Hebrews 10:1-18 - **The New Covenant is the reality.**

12. 2 Corinthians 3:13 - The Old Covenant is a covered glory,
The New Covenant is glory uncovered.

13. Hebrews 7:23-28 - The Old Covenant had many high priests,
The New Covenant has only one high priest. (Jesus Christ)

14. Hebrews 5:1-4 - The Old Covenant had earthly priests,
Hebrews 9:24, 10:12 - **The New Covenant has a heavenly priest.**

15. Hebrews 7:12;28 - The Old Covenant makes priests by law,
The New Covenant makes priests by oath.

16.   Hebrews 9:2 - The Old Covenant had an earthly tabernacle,
Hebrews 8:2 - **The New Covenant has a heavenly tabernacle.**

17.   Hebrews 7:11,21 - The Old Covenant priesthood was in the lineage of
       Aaron (Aaron priest hood),
The New Covenant priesthood is in the Melchizedek lineage. (Melchizedek priesthood)

18.   Hebrews 5:1-4 - The Old Covenant priests were sinners,
Hebrews 7:26 - **The New Covenant priest has no sin.**

19.   Matthew 5:17-18 - The Old Covenant was fulfilled,
Hebrews 8:6, 10:9 - **The New Covenant is now enforced.**

20.   Jeremiah 31:33 - The Old Covenant, the law was written in stone tablets.
The New Covenant, the law is written in people's hearts.

21.   The Old Covenant demanded dead works,
The New Covenant only demands obedience through faith.

22.   The Old Covenant - Moses and prophets were mediators,
The New Covenant - Jesus Christ is the mediator.

23.   The Old Covenant needed offerings for sin,
The New Covenant, Jesus is the perfect sin offering.

24.   The Old Covenant needed statutes and ordinances,
The New Covenant only needs one's heart.

25.   The Old Covenant - the tabernacle was made with hands,
The New Covenant - the tabernacle is made without hands.

26.   The Old Covenant - remembrance of sin was done yearly,
The New Covenant - forgiveness and washing away of sin was done once and for all.

27.   Hebrews 10:3 - The Old Covenant remembers sin,
Hebrews 8:12. 10:17 **The New Covenant does not remember sin.**

28.   2 Corinthians 3:6-7 - The Old Covenant is a ministry of death,
The New Covenant is a ministry of life.

29.   Deuteronomy 4: 7-8 - The Old Covenant is for Israelites by birth only,
Luke 22:20 - **The New Covenant is for all men who believe.**

14 Scriptures On <u>Repentance</u> *Before* <u>Forgiveness</u>

1. Luke 17:3-4

"If your brother sins, rebuke him, and if he repents, forgive him, and if he sins against you seven times in the day, and turns to you seven times, saying, 'I repent,' you must forgive him".

2. 1 John 1:9

"If we confess our sins, He is faithful to forgive us our sins…"

3. Acts 5:31

"He is the one whom God exalted to His right hand as a Prince and a Savior, to grant repentance to Israel, and forgiveness of sins."

4. Acts 17:30

"Therefore having overlooked the times of ignorance, God is now declaring to men that all people everywhere should repent,"

5. Acts 3:19

"Therefore repent and return, so that your sins may be wiped away, in order that times of refreshing may come from the presence of the Lord;"

6. Luke 13:3

"I tell you, no, but unless you repent, you will all likewise perish."

7. 2 Peter 3:9

"The Lord is not slow about His promise, as some count slowness, but is patient toward you, not wishing for any to perish but for all to come to repentance."

8. Revelation 3:19

"Those whom I love, I reprove and discipline; therefore be zealous and repent."

9. Mark 1:4

"John the Baptist appeared in the wilderness preaching a baptism of repentance for the forgiveness of sins."

10. Revelation 2:20-21

"But I have *this* against you, that you tolerate* the woman Jezebel, who calls herself a prophetess, and she teaches and leads My bond-servants astray so that they commit *acts of immorality* and eat things sacrificed to idols. I gave her time to repent, and she does not want to repent of her immorality." *(Strongs 863) - "forgive"

11. Joel 2:13

"Rip your heart to pieces [in sorrow and contrition] and not your garments." Now return [in repentance] to the LORD your God, For He is gracious and compassionate, Slow to anger, abounding in loving kindness [faithful to His covenant with His people]; And He relents [His sentence of] evil [when His people genuinely repent]."

12. Revelation 2:5

"So remember *the heights* from which you have fallen, and repent [change your inner self—your old way of thinking, your sinful behavior—seek God's will] and do the works you did at first [when you first knew Me]; otherwise, I will visit you and remove your lampstand (the church, its impact) from its place—unless you repent."

13. Luke 24:46-47

"and He said to them, "Thus it is written, that the Christ would suffer and rise again from the dead the third day, and that repentance for forgiveness of sins would be proclaimed in His name to all the nations, beginning from Jerusalem."

14. Acts 2:38

"Peter *said* to them, "Repent, and each of you be baptized in the name of Jesus Christ for the forgiveness of your sins; and you will receive the gift of the Holy Spirit."

Q: Does Jesus forgive anyone who refuses to repent? Should We?

_____

_____

_____

Ephesians 4:15
"but <u>speaking the truth</u> *in love*, we are to **grow up in all *aspects* into Him** who is the head, *even* Christ"

Rather than enabling people to continue sinning by telling them that they are forgiven without repentance, we should speak the truth to them. That is how the Holy Spirit can convict them of the wrong they are doing. That is being a mature Son like Jesus. "Go, and sin no more."

<u>After</u> they have repented, (turned from their ways) they will be forgiven, and restored.

Our job is that we live a life without *bitterness*.

Mark 11:25 indicates that Jesus is saying ***not to hold bitterness against anyone.***

Mark 11:26 was added, and is not scripture.

We should forgive others the same way that God forgives them, not any different.

Declaring The <u>Sonship</u> Book (Ephesians)

I am an ambassador for Christ Jesus - Ephesians 1:1

I have been given every spiritual blessing in heavenly places in Christ - Ephesians 1:3

I am holy and without blemish before God - Ephesians 1:4

I have been redeemed through Jesus's blood - Ephesians 1:7

I know the will of God in Christ Jesus- Ephesians 1:9

My inheritance is in Christ - Ephesians 1:11

I have been sealed with the Spirit of promise, the Holy Spirit - Ephesians 1:13

I have the Spirit of wisdom and revelation in the knowledge of Him - Ephesians 1:17

I know what is the hope He has called me to, and what is the riches of His glorious inheritance to me - Ephesians 1:18

I am alive in Christ, and seated with Him in heavenly places far above all principalities, and every name that is named - Ephesians 2:6

Through the cross of Jesus Christ I have been reconciled back to God, by one Spirit into the presence of the Father - Ephesians 2:18

I am a permanent dwelling place of God by the Spirit - Ephesians 2:22

I am a joint heir in Christ Jesus and fellow partaker of His promise - Ephesians 3:6

My power is limitless, because it is the same measure of Christ's power. Therefore I give life freely.

I have been granted the wealth of His glory and power and I am strengthened in the Spirit in the inward man - Ephesians 3:16

I know experientially what is the love of Christ and I am filled up with the measure of the fullness of God - Ephesians 3:19

I walk in a manner worthy of the call in Christ - Ephesians 4:1

I have been given the same measure of grace that Christ was given - Ephesians 4:7

I am not a child, tossed to and fro with every wind of doctrine and the deceitfulness of this world - Ephesians 4:14

I speak the truth in love so that we all grow up in all aspects into Christ - Ephesians 4:15

I lay aside the old self, I am renewed in the spirit of my mind; and I have put on the new self that looks like God - Ephesians 4:22-24

I have righteous anger for the things not of God and I am without sin - Ephesians 4:26

When I speak it is simple and edifies all who hear - Ephesians 4:29

I am kind and tender hearted to those around me.

The same way that God in Christ forgave me is the way that I forgive them - Ephesians 4:32

I am an imitator of my Father in heaven; I look and act as He does - Ephesians 5:1

As I walk in love as Christ to others, it is as a fragrant aroma, the sacrifice of obedience to God - Ephesians 5:2

I do not participate in or enable unfruitful works of darkness, instead I expose them - Ephesians 5:11

I work efficiently, I do not waste time - Ephesians 5:16

I am fully clothed with the armor of God, so I resist the devil, like a good soldier I stand firm in the faith - Ephesians 6:13

David Lage's 7 Absolutes

1. **Be like Christ in all ways, like Jesus**

    "until we all reach unity in the faith and in the knowledge of the Son of God, as we mature to the full measure of the stature of Christ." (Ephesians 4:13)

    "Instead, speaking the truth in love, we will in all things grow up into Christ Himself, who is the head." (Ephesians 4:15)

2. **If you teach a different gospel than the one Jesus taught, you should be accursed.**

    "But even though we, or an angel from heaven, should preach to you a gospel contrary to that which we have preached to you, let him be accursed." (Galatians 1:8)

    "I am afraid, however, that just as Eve was deceived by the serpent's cunning, your minds may be led astray from your simple and pure devotion to Christ. For if someone comes and proclaims a Jesus other than the One we proclaimed, or if you receive a different spirit than the One you received, or a different gospel than the one you accepted, you put up with it way too easily." (2 Corinthians 11:3-4)

3. **You are to follow knowing, and trusting only the will of God.**

    "For the word of God is living and active and sharper than any two-edged sword, and piercing as far as the division of soul and spirit, of both joints and marrow, and able to judge the thoughts and intentions of the heart." Hebrews (4:12)

    "I can do nothing on My own initiative. As I hear, I judge; and My judgment is just, because I do not seek My own will, but the will of Him who sent Me." (John 5:30)

    "I am convinced that the effect of his touch within you is permanent; this is the Christ-anointing that teaches you all things, so that you do not need any teacher whose doctrine does not resonate with truth. Deception cannot compete with spirit-resonance." (1 John 2:27)

4. **Don't worry about what to say. The Holy Spirit will fill your mouth when you get there.**

   "So make up your mind not to worry beforehand how to defend yourselves. For I will give you speech and wisdom that none of your adversaries will be able to resist or contradict." (Luke 21:14-15)

5. **If you don't teach healing, you're not preaching the gospel.**

   "As you go, preach this message: '- The kingdom of heaven is near.' Heal the sick, raise the dead, cleanse the lepers, drive out demons. Freely you have received; freely give." (Matthew 10:7-8)

   "For I am not ashamed of the gospel of Christ: for it is the power of God unto salvation to every one that believeth; to the Jew first, and also to the Greek." (Romans 1:16)
   "I don't preach with eloquent words but a demonstration of the Holy Spirit and power" (1 Corinthians 2:1)

6. **If God tells you to lie, cheat, or steal, you know it's not the real God.**

   "You belong to your father, the devil, and you want to carry out his desires. He was a murderer from the beginning, refusing to uphold the truth, because there is no truth in him. When he lies, he speaks his native language, because he is a liar and the father of lies." (John 8:44)

   "So I tell you this, and testify to it in the Lord: You must no longer walk as the Gentiles do, in the futility of their thinking. They are darkened in their understanding and alienated from the life of God because of the ignorance that is in them due to the hardness of their hearts. Having lost all sense of shame, they have given themselves over to sensuality for the practice of every kind of impurity, with a craving for more. But this is not the way you came to know Christ. Surely you heard of Him and were taught in Him in keeping with the truth that is in Jesus. You were taught to put off your former way of life, your old self, which is being corrupted by its deceitful desires; to be renewed in the spirit of your minds; and to put on the new self, created to be like God in true righteousness and holiness. Therefore each of you must put off falsehood and speak truthfully to his neighbor, for we are members of one another. "Be angry, yet do not sin." Do not let the sun set upon your anger, and do not give the devil a foothold. He who has been stealing must steal no longer, but must work, doing good with his own hands, that he may have something to share with the one in need. Let no unwholesome talk come out of your mouths, but only what is helpful for building up the one in need and bringing grace to those who listen. And do not grieve the Holy Spirit of God, in whom you were sealed for the day of redemption. Get rid of all bitterness, rage and anger, outcry and slander, along with every form of malice." (Ephesians 4:17-31)

"Do you not know that the unrighteous will not inherit the kingdom of God? Do not be deceived; neither the immoral, nor idolaters, nor adulterers, nor sexual perverts, nor thieves, nor the greedy, nor drunkards, nor revilers, nor robbers will inherit the kingdom of God." (1 Corinthians 6:9-10)

7. **It's never a carnal answer.**

   "How God anointed Jesus of Nazareth with the Holy Spirit and with power, and how Jesus went around doing good and healing all who were oppressed by the devil, because God was with Him." (Acts 10:38)

   "For we wrestle not against flesh and blood, but against principalities, against powers, against the rulers of the darkness of this world, against spiritual wickedness in high places." (Ephesians 6:12)

Correct Answers For Section Prompts

Page 4
Q: Give examples of planting a seed of faith:
A:

1. Speaking the Word of God over every area of life.
2. Confessing who I am in Christ.
3. Commanding any block from God's will to GO!
   1 John 4:17, Deuteronomy 30:19, Proverbs 18:21, Hebrews 4:12

Page 5
Q: Paul is referring to satan as 'the god of this world.' How did satan get that position?
A: Adam and Eve *turned* the position of 'god of this world' over to satan by obeying him instead of God.
   Genesis 3, 2 Corinthians 4:4, Romans 6:16, 2 Corinthians 11:3, 1 Timothy 2:13-14

Page 6
   Sin = Death
   Obedience = Life
   Romans 8

Page 7
Q: What consequences come to us today from seeking knowledge over obedience to God?
A:

1. Spiritual death.
2. Always learning and never coming to the experiential knowledge of the truth.
3. Leaning on your own understanding.
4. Head knowledge without power.
5. Deceiving yourself by continually learning instead of being Jesus to the world.
6. To know to do good and not do it is a sin.
   Romans 6:23, 2 Timothy 3:7, Proverbs 3:5-6, James 1:23, James 4:17

Page 7

Q: What was God's original plan for Adam and Eve:

A:

1. To be like God.
2. The be the **g**od of this world.
3. To collaborate with God.
4. To have authority & dominion, rule over the earth.
5. Be fruitful and multiply.
6. Freedom from pain, sickness, disease, lack, and hardship.
7. Eternal life.

Genesis 1-2, John 10:34-35

Page 9

Q: Why was it illegal for God to take rulership when He saw the fall of mankind?

A: Because God cannot lie, and He decreed that the rulership of earth was given to man.

Numbers 23:19, Genesis 1:26-28

Page 9

Q: How did the blood covenant between God and Abraham provide God access back into this world?

A: God had to find a man that was willing to give up everything he had, so that God could legally give everything HE had, even unto the death of His own Son. Abraham's actions of faith released God to work in the earth through Abraham's legal dominion.

Genesis 22:16-17

Page 12

Q: Why was Mary's verbal declaration necessary for the conception of Jesus?

A:

1. Her word was the seed of the Word of God.
2. The Word she spoke in faith with her dominion brought forth human life inside her.

Hebrews 11, Genesis 3:15, 1 Peter 1:23, John 1:14

Page 14

Q: Jesus said the Spirit of the Lord is upon Him because:

A:

    1.   Because God anointed Jesus to preach the gospel to the poor. He was sent to proclaim release to the captives, and recovery of sight to the blind.

    2.   He was sent to set free those who are oppressed, and to proclaim the favorable year of the Lord.

Luke 4:18-19

Page 14

Q: Jesus had to come to the earth as a ____ in order that He would have the ____ God assigned to man. It was not until He was ____ when ___ that Jesus had the ability of God on the earth.

A: man, dominion, anointed, baptized

John 5:26-27, Genesis 1:26-28, Luke 3:21-23, Luke 4:18-19

Page 15

Q: Jesus was God in the flesh. So, why would God have to anoint Him with The Holy Ghost and with power?

A: Because He laid aside His divinity to be born here. When He walked on the earth, Jesus was fully man.

Philippians 2:6-8, Hebrews 4:15

Page 17

Q: Give examples of when and how Jesus demonstrated His authority and power here on earth.

A:

    1.   He casted out devils and healed the sick.

    2.   He commanded the storm to be still.

    3.   He drove out the money changers in the temple.

    4.   He multiplied food.

Luke 4:35-44, Matthew 8:23-27, Matthew 21:12, Mark 11:15, Matthew 14:13-21

Page 19

Q: Give examples of how we make satan God's footstool

A:

1.   Identify the works of the devil. (Sickness, disease, lack, poverty, destruction, depression, and anything that doesn't look like heaven)

2.   Utilize walking in faith (authority and dominion) to get the works of satan off of people, and enforce the victory over the devil in Jesus' name.

John 10:10, 1 John 3:8, James 4:17, 1 John 4:17

Page 21

Q: Even though the disciples did not have Holy Ghost power in them before the day of Pentecost, describe how they were able to heal and set people free:

A:

1.   The disciples operated in the delegated authority of Jesus by faith in Him.

2.   By the stripes that Jesus WOULD take, every person's freedom was paid for.

Matthew 10:1. Luke 10:17, Isaiah 53:5, 1 Peter 2:24

Page 22

Q: How can we do the 'greater works' referred to in John 14:12:

A:

1.   The devil is now a defeated enemy.

2.   The Holy Spirit was poured out on the day of Pentecost unlimited!

Colossians 2:15, Acts 2

Page 24

Q: What was Jesus referring to as being finished?

A:

1. The Old Covenant.
2. The Law.
3. Jesus broke ALL curses.

We have all the benefits of the Old Covenant + those of the New Covenant without any curses.

John 19:28-30, Hebrews 8:13, Hebrews 9:12, 26, Galatians 3:13

Page 25

Q: Where in scripture does the New Covenant begin?

A:

    1.   The New Covenant began on the day of Pentecost when the spirit was poured out on all flesh and they began speaking with new tongues.

Acts 2, John 14:17, Matthew 26:28, John 19:30

Page 25

Q: Upon His resurrection Jesus received ALL authority. How much authority does satan / demons have now here on earth?

A:

    1.   They have NO authority. People allow the devil to work through them illegally.

Matthew 28:18, 1 John 3:8, Hebrews 2:14-15, Luke 10:18

Page 27

Q: What 'miracles and signs' are evident in New Covenant Baptisms?

A:

    1.   When sons of God baptize people by faith, the result is that sons of God are reproduced.

    2.   Everything that's not of God stays in the water.

    3.   The person's life is new and changed going forward.

    4.   Healing.

    5.   Deliverance.

    6.   Baptism of the Holy Ghost.

    7.   Prophetic words given and received.

    8.   Slain in the spirit.

Romans 6:4, Mark 16:16, 2 Corinthians 5:17, Acts 2:38, Acts 19:5-6

Page 28

Q: What must man do to operate in the authority of Jesus?

A: Only believe by putting action to their faith in Jesus (put a demand on the anointing) and don't stop until you get the promise (all Gods promises were are already established as yes and Amen)

Mark 5:36, Hebrews 10:36, 1 John 2:27

Page 28

Q: What have Believers been commissioned to do?

A:

1. Lay hands on the sick
2. Set the captives free
3. Cleanse the lepers
4. Baptize those who believe
5. Preach the gospel
6. Make disciples
7. Cast out demons
8. Speak in new tongues

Matthew 28:18-20, Mark 16:15-18

Page 30

Q: How does a Believer get baptized with the Holy Spirit?

A: Same way you get healed- put a demand on the anointing; believe and speak out the promise until you receive it. Scripture says that through your belly flows rivers of living water; declare that the Holy Spirit fills and flows through the Believer and instruct them to begin making sounds and the Holy Spirit will then help them to begin speaking in new tongues.

John 7:38-39, Ephesians 2:8-9, 1 Corinthians 1:27-28, 1 Corinthians 14,
Matthew 7:8-11, Hebrews 11:1,6, Ephesians 6:18

Page 31

Q: What is referred to in scripture as 'new tongues'?; when is it given to a believer and for what purpose?

A: 'New Tongues' is a Private prayer language also referred to as your Heavenly language- which is given to a believer in Jesus Christ upon infilling of the Holy Spirit. Speaking in tongues is direct connection with God that is not understood by satan and stirs a believer in their faith. It is stated in Ephesians that praying in the Spirit is the way we utilize the full armor of God.

Ephesians 6:18 Romans 8:27

Page 31

Q: What signs shall follow those who believe in Jesus?

A:

1. They will lay hands on the sick and they shall recover.
2. They will cast out demons.
3. They can drink/ eat anything and it will not affect them.
4. They will speak in new tongues.
5. Believer knows the finished work in Christ Jesus

Mark 16:15-18

Page 34

Q: What characteristics encompass living by faith as a New Creation in Christ?

A: Everything of the old is gone. Everything Jesus is you are, and everything Jesus has you have. You are seated in heavenly places and live from the point of victory!

2 Corinthians 5:17-18, Ephesians 4:7, 1 John 4:17, Ephesians 1:3, Ephesians 2:6, Romans 8:17,37

Page 35

Q: What must we do to make God's enemy (satan) His footstool?

A: Applying the authority given to believers by Jesus to do The Great Commission to put all things in subjection under His feet. It is Jesus' authority that He gives to believers to use - no 'wrong' action of a believer can give Jesus' authority over to the devil.

Ephesians 1:22, Hebrews 2:8

Page 38

Q: Give examples of Sons of God demonstrating God's power.

A:

1. Walking by the Spirit
2. Speaking those things that are not (in the natural) as though they are and knowing they will change. (ie: supernatural childbirth- no pain)
3. Laying hands on the sick for healing, salvation and deliverance.
4. Speaking to 'mountains' and believing they will move.

Galatians 5:16, Romans 4:17, Luke 13:13, Mark 11:23-24, Luke 8:24, Acts 10:38

Page 40

Q: What does scripture tell us about seeking the favor of man?

A: Scripture tells us that if we strive to please man we can not truly serve Christ and that we are not fit for the Kingdom of God. The motivation behind why we do all things must be in line with the life of Jesus and to serve Him in all ways.

Galatians 6:1-10, Acts 5:29, 1 Thessalonians 2:4, John 12:42-43

Page 41

Q: What does scripture say happens to us if we 'Add to or take away from' the Word? (Jesus is the Word made flesh)

A: If we add to or take away from the word we will be held accountable with severe consequences (doubly accursed) and we will be unstable in all our ways.

Revelation 22:18-19, 1 Timothy 1:3-7, Galatians 1:6-10

Page 43

Q: What does scripture tell us about being 'double minded'?

A: If we have "one foot in the old covenant and one foot in the new covenant" the work of Christ is distorted, back and forth from being finished to not yet completed. This 'double- mindedness' makes one unstable in ALL their ways.

James 1:8, Galatians 3

Page 44

Q: How does a Believer have the mind of Christ?

A: When we repent (turn from our sinful nature) and accept Christ Jesus as our Lord we are a new creation in Him. As a new creation we have the mind of Christ.

1 Corinthians 5:17, 1 Corinthians 2:16

Page 45

Q: Describe the difference in Old Covenant "begging" prayers vs. New Covenant declarations:

A: Old Covenant prayers include waiting on God, asking Him to do something, and giving Him reasons why He should do it.

New Covenant declarations are commanding problems to go, based on confidence in the finished work of Jesus. It is not even talking to God about the problem. You simply command, and see the manifestation of obedience to your word. One is asking God to do what He has already done, and commanded you to do. The other is operating as a mature Son of God, calling those things that are not as though they are with faith for them to manifest.

1 Corinthians 2:9-10, Hebrews 1:1-4, Mark 16:15-18, Mark 11:23, Romans 4:17

Page 48
Q: Describe the nature of God:
A: Healer. Restorer. Redeemer. Savior. Liberator. Loving. Gracious. Merciful. Self-sacrificing. Strong. Promise keeper. Faithful to His Word. Trustworthy. Light. Eternally powerful.

Romans 1:20, 1 John 1:5, 1 John 4:8,

Page 49
Q: Sin leads to _____ which leads to death.
A: sickness

Romans 8

Page 50
Q: Where is Jesus, The Holy Spirit, and the Father?
A: Scripturally, they are in heaven, and in us, and we are also in heaven and here. Jesus comes to dwell in you when you get born again. When you get the baptism of the Holy Ghost, you get the Holy Spirit. Jesus said that He AND the Father would dwell in you. We are seated with Christ in heavenly places.

Hebrews 1:3, 13, 2 Corinthians 3:17, Acts 1:8, John 14:23, Ephesians 2:6

Page 52
Q: What does the idiom 'Thorn in the flesh' really mean?
A: English speakers would say, "pain in the neck." Biblically, this is always in reference to a people group or person who is continually bothersome.

Numbers 33:55, Joshua 23:13

Page 54
Q: Did Paul ever overcome any of satan's messenger's?
A: Yes. (Bar-Jesus) Paul got fed up with the devil in the false prophet, and took his authority, overcoming the distraction.

Acts 13:6-12

Page 57
Q: What effect did the devil have on Job?
A: The devil stole from Job. He destroyed Job's land, his livestock, his family and his body.

Job 1:13-19, Job 2:7-8

Page 57
Q: What effect did God have on Job?
A: God restored what Job had lost. He increased Job's possessions %100.

Job 42:10,12-14

Page 60
Q: What is God's will for our lives?
A: God wants us to use our free will to **enforce His authority** on earth in our own lives and the lives of others. This authority is the power to drive out every influence of the devil so that we live in complete freedom. This is the Great Commission.

Mark 16:15-20, Matthew 28:16-20

Page 64
Q: What does Galatians 3:13 state?
A: "Christ redeemed us from the curse of the Law, having become a curse for us—for it is written, "Cursed is everyone who hangs on a tree."
The only curse a person can have put on them is one that they wrongly believe can be put on them. Don't make the mistake of falsely quoting old covenant scriptures putting yourself back under the curse of the law. Jesus abolished all curses and believers are hidden in Him - protected from evil.

Page 67
Q: What does Jesus commission us to do in order to mature?
A: Scripture tells us that when we are only hearers of the Word we deceive ourselves.
We must DO the will of God; Heal the sick, raise the dead, cast out demons, speak in new tongues, baptize others, and duplicate more disciples in order that we have a strong foundation in Jesus and mature into Him in ALL ways.

James 1:22-25, Matthew 7:24-27, John 4:34, Acts 10:38, 1 John 3:8, 1 John 4:17

Page 70

Q: Is Jesus with you, or not?

A: When you accept Jesus as Lord He lives in you and will never leave you nor forsake you.

Matthew 28:20, Galatians 2:20, 1 John 2:27, John 14:15-31

Page 74

Q: What is Faith?

A: Faith is acting in accordance of our beliefs in Jesus by implementing His Authority and Dominion He has provided us here on earth.

Hebrews 11:1-3, Mark 11:22-23, Psalms 33:8-9, Luke 17:6

Page 78

Q: How does a Believer in Jesus receive His anointing?

A: Become a born again believer in Jesus!

Acts 2:38, Acts 1:8, Ephesians 8:26

Page 79

Q: What other scriptures show us that Jesus healed them all?

A: "how God anointed Jesus of Nazareth with the Holy Spirit and with power, who went about doing good and healing all who were oppressed by the devil, for God was with Him."

Acts 10:38 Matt. 4:23-24; 8:16-17; 9:35; 12:15; 14:14, 34-36; 15:30; 19:2; and 21:14

Page 81

Q: What is the difference between the wise man and the foolish man?

A: Scripture tells us that both the foolish and the wise man heard the Word of Jesus; the difference between the two was the foolish man did nothing after hearing the Word and the wise man took action. The foolish man was called a fool with a house built on sand (unable to withstand any storm); the wise man on the other hand took action in line with the Words Jesus said and had a foundation of solid rock! The difference between being foolish or wise is in taking action!! Be a doer of God's word!

Matthew 7:24-27, James 1:22-25

Page 83

Q: How does a Believer 'resist the devil'?

A: We must walk in obedience to ALL we are commanded by Jesus to do and be. Recognizing when something is of God or is of the enemy is critical; it is by the inward witness, the Holy Spirit within us that we are to judge all things. The things that are of God will never go against the Word of God nor the finished work of Jesus! (Remember Jesus IS the Word of God made flesh.) The devil will often enter into a person's life through fear and greed; we must only want what is of God.

> 2 Corinthians 11:14, James 4:7-8, Ephesians 6:11, Romans 6:16, John 10:10, Hebrews 5:14, 1 Corinthians 2:15

Page 86

Q: Why does Paul say there is a better way than operating in the 'gifts of the Holy Spirit?'

A: Jesus restored man's position of authority here on earth. When we operate in His authority ALL the 'gifts of the Spirit' follow / flow and we can walk in the **full** power Jesus provided us as believers. 1 Corinthians 13 is 'The Love Chapter.' Jesus perfectly embodied love and demonstrated love by operating in authority and dominion all of His life to set the captives free.

> John 15:2, Ephesians 1:3, 4:7, 1 Corinthians 13, John 15:13

Page 86

Q: How does the Holy Spirit equip Believers to do the Word of God?

A: Upon a believer being filled with the Holy Spirit - the Spirit of God dwells in them. He gives Believers the same anointing of Jesus.
The Holy Spirit IS the GIFT that empowers a Son of God to walk in the Spirit and operate in the fullness of everything Jesus commissioned us to.

> Romans 8:11,26, Isaiah 11:2, Acts 1:8,

Page 88

Q: What fruits of the Spirit do words of life bare?
A: "The fruit of the Spirit is love, joy, peace, patience, kindness, generosity, faithfulness, gentleness, self-control..."
Words of life put into motion all the promises of God.
Words (seeds) that are in-line with the will of God produce life (words / actions that edify the body of Christ to grow more into the likeness of Jesus everyday) To love like Christ one must utilize Holy Spirit wisdom when speaking truth as we are required to rebuke and correct those who are out of the will of God.

Galatians 5:22-23, Proverbs 18:21, Ephesians 6:17

Page 88

Q: Give examples of speaking life versus death.
A:

1. LIFE - I believe the report of God. I am healed.
   Death - I have an incurable disease.

2. LIFE - I can do all things through Christ who strengthens me.
   Death - I can't change.

3. LIFE - Jesus took all my pain away so that I wouldn't bare any.
   Death - My back is killing me.

4. LIFE - I have the mind of Christ.
   Death - I'm not tech-savy enough to figure this out.

5. LIFE - I'm holding you accountable to do what's right. You're better than this lifestyle.
   Death - I don't want to judge, so just do what you feel is best. God will love you anyway.

1 Peter 2:24, Philippians 4:13, Matthew 8:17, 1 Corinthians 2:16, Romans 6:23, Galatians 6:1-2

Page 90

Q: Give additional examples of personalizing scripture to speak over yourself and the lives of your loved ones.

A: My family is saved in Jesus' name! By His stripes, I <u>was</u> healed! I do not lack anything. I always have more than enough to meet my needs, and to give to those around me.

2 Peter 3:9, 1 Peter 2:24, Philippians 4:19

Page 92

Q: Give examples of making yourself accessible and available.

A: Budget time to mister when you go to the marketplace and be aware of your surroundings. Actively engage with people to find the needs they have, be moved with compassion like Jesus. Be ready to step out in boldness to release the power of the kingdom to set the captives free. Provide those whom you minister to with ways to connect with you (ie: phone, email, scheduled group activities) in the future. Be organized, respond to requests and follow up.

Luke 19:10

Page 97

Q: Give an example of speaking out - declaring for somebody's miracle.

A: "You will live and not die!" (raising the dead)

Mark 11:23, Romans 4:17

Page 111

Q: Does Jesus forgive anyone who refuses to repent? Should We?

A: No. Jesus does not forgive sinners in rebelion. He requires change (repentance) before receiving someone in a restored relationship. We should follow His example, and hold people accountable in order that they may be reconciled back to Christ. Scripture tells us not to hold bitterness, no matter what choices others make. At the same time, true forgiveness can <u>only</u> come as a result of true repentance.

Revelation 2:20-21, Luke 17:3-4

I declare that every word in this book is an anointed instruction that you will live by. It is the Word of God. Hear it, act on it, and go teach someone else to walk in freedom too. That's the true gospel, and it is the only one that always works.

Hannah Ferguson,
Ordained Minister, Author
su.hannahf@gmail.com (417) 527-5645

Declaring everybody walks in the freedom and authority provided to us by Jesus, in obedience to Him, by being a doer of the Word of God!

Amy Melrose, BSN
Ordained Minister, Author
amymelrose@aol.com (760) 622-9438

My favorite is declaring over pregnant ladies. I want to see babies and their mothers healed and whole with no pain during the entire pregnancy and birthing process as a testimony of God's power. I started out just speaking over women to have supernatural labor, and I saw results with women having pain-free childbirth. Then God revealed to me that since some babies needed to be healed in the womb, I needed to declare over them so that they didn't have to be born with sickness, disease or birth defects. I also declare for mothers to have no complications, no baby blues, and that the babies sleep well. Lastly, I speak that the Holy Spirit touch them from the inside out. That means mama and baby both get filled with the Holy Spirit! I encourage every believer to also speak over pregnant ladies. They are usually very grateful, and we do see the Word of God come to pass.

Patricia Lage, Ordained Minister
Dave Lage, Ordained Minister (515) 297-3577

I used to believe that sitting in the closet, listening for a voice in my head was the gospel. Now I live by the revelation that obedience is the greatest form of worship. The best advice I could give you would be, "Go! Be Jesus to the world and nothing less."

Ruth Ferguson,
Ordained Minister

Made in the USA
Las Vegas, NV
07 May 2023

71678279R00077